THE CRAFTER'S GUIDE TO
PRICING YOUR WORK

The Crafter's Guide to
PRICING YOUR WORK

DAN RAMSEY

BETTERWAY BOOKS

CINCINNATI, OHIO

The Crafter's Guide to Pricing Your Work. Copyright © 1997 by Dan Ramsey. Printed and bound in the United States of America. All rights reserved. No part of this book may be reproduced in any form or by any electronic or mechanical means including information storage and retrieval systems without permission in writing from the publisher, except by a reviewer, who may quote brief passages in a review. Published by Betterway Books, an imprint of F&W Publications, Inc., 1507 Dana Ave., Cincinnati, Ohio 45207. (800) 289-0963. First edition.

Other fine Betterway Books are available from your local bookstore or direct from the publisher.

01 00 99 98 97 5 4 3 2 1

Library of Congress Cataloging-in-Publication Data

Ramsey, Dan
    The crafter's guide to pricing your work / by Dan Ramsey.
        p.   cm.
    Includes index.
    ISBN 1-55870-435-3 (alk. paper)
    1. Handicraft—Prices. 2. Selling—Handicraft. 3. Handicraft industries—
  Management. 4. Pricing. I. Title.
HF5439.H27R36 1997
745.5'068'8—dc21   96-47285
                                                        CIP

Content edited by Perri Weinberg-Schenker
Production edited by Patrick Souhan
Cover photography by Erik Von Fischer/Blink Photography
Shirt by Sheryl Ball and Deniele Croissant for Duncan Enterprises
Basket by Dorothy Egan
Birdhouse by Judith Hawn
Frame by Donna Malone and Kenna Reynolds
Holiday boxes and cloth background by Ursula Roma

"I have filled him with the Spirit of God, with skill, ability and knowledge in all kinds of crafts—to make artistic designs for work in gold, silver and bronze, to cut and set stones, to work in wood, and to engage in all kinds of craftsmanship."
(Exodus 31:3-5 NIV)

Acknowledgments

Writing a book is a craft. It requires materials, tools and techniques. Most important, it requires resources. Thanks so much to the resources who helped craft this book: Bernadette Finnerty of *The Crafts Report*; Helise Benjamin of the American Craft Association; the Hobby Industry Association; Rick Rochon of Olor Enterprises; Sharon Mast of The Myrtlewood Gallery; Nancy Bartow of Scholfield Valley Wood Products; Ian Bowen, Thomas Clark and Dan MacAlpine of *Woodshop News*; David Lewis of Betterway Books; and Lori Capps of the Business Development Center at Southwest Oregon Community College. A special thanks is extended to the craftspeople and sysops on CompuServe's Handcrafts, Fibercrafts and Sewing & Quilting Forums who offered their pricing ideas and experiences online.

In addition, the author thanks the U.S. Small Business Administration, Office of Business Development; Service Corps of Retired Executives, Portland, Oregon, District Office; U.S. Department of Commerce, Office of Business Liaison and Minority Business Development Agency; Internal Revenue Service; and the staff of Ramsey Business Strategies.

Thanks, too, to the many magazines that inspire and serve craftspeople: *American Craft, The Artist's Magazine, Cast On, Ceramic Arts & Crafts, Country Needlecraft, Crafts Magazine, Crafts 'n Things, The Crafts Report, Craftworks, Decorative Artist's Workbook, Fiberarts, Lapidary Journal, Michael's Arts & Crafts, PaintWorks, Professional Stained Glass, Profitable Craft Merchandising, Sew Business, Sideline Business, Threads Magazine, Women's Circle, The Workbasket* and many others.

Business forms in this book were created using PerFORM Forms Designer from Symantec/Delrina.

Names, addresses, telephone numbers and related information are included in this book for the convenience of the reader and were current when this book was written. No endorsement is implied.

TABLE OF CONTENTS

CHAPTER FOUR

How to Price Ceramic Crafts

CHAPTER FIVE

How to Price Jewelry and Metal Crafts

CHAPTER SIX

How to Price Fine Arts

CHAPTER SEVEN

How to Increase Profits Without Reducing Quality

Introduction

Crafting is an enjoyable hobby. It can also be an expensive one. If you'd like to cover your craft expenses—and make a few extra dollars—without sacrificing your independence, *The Crafter's Guide to Pricing Your Work* by Dan Ramsey is for you. You'll learn how professionals in every craft field set their prices and sell their products. You'll also learn how to sell the value of your work so that the price is less important. And you'll learn how to increase your profits without sacrificing the quality of your work—or your enjoyment of crafts.

Chapter one introduces you to the craft of pricing. Like any other craft, pricing has raw materials, tools, techniques and a finished product. This chapter introduces these components of pricing and illustrates each point so you can easily apply them to your crafts. It covers estimating material costs, labor, overhead and profit. It also shows you how to sell the value of your work, how to negotiate and how to increase your prices. It even explains why prices are different from region to region—and what to do about it.

Chapters two through six apply the basics of pricing to more than seventy-five crafts. Chapter two covers pricing popular crafts such as decorative painting and woodcraft. Chapter three explains pricing needle and fabric crafts. Chapter four is about pricing a wide variety of ceramics. Chapter five covers pricing jewelry and metal crafts. Chapter six explains how to price fine arts. Each chapter applies pricing rules to specific projects illustrating how to price your crafts. It covers costing materials, setting studio rates, estimating overhead and ensuring profit for your work. In each chapter, you'll get *specific* pricing recommendations to make your crafts competitive and profitable.

Finally, chapter seven offers proven methods of how to effectively market and profit from what you make. You will learn from the experiences of dozens of successful crafters. It covers recordkeeping, selling at craft shows and flea markets, consignment sales, mail-order sales, how to reduce material costs, and making your craft studio more efficient. It also includes advanced techniques for making your crafts pay for themselves: managing cash flow, building repeat business, getting valuable advice, paying taxes and enjoying what you do.

Author Dan Ramsey is president of Ramsey Business Strategies, a business consulting service that specializes in helping small businesses grow. Throughout this book he offers proven pricing formulas, practical business practices and case histories, all explaining how to profitably price your work.

The studio rates recommended in this book are based on interviews with successful working crafters in a variety of fields. From these interviews a matrix of typical studio rates was developed based on the creativity of the crafter, uniqueness of the design, the relative skills required to execute the products, the craft tools needed, the popularity of the craft and the value perceived by the consumer. This matrix was used to develop the studio rates recommended in this book.

The Crafter's Guide to Pricing Your Work also includes a glossary that clearly defines common pricing and marketing terms such as consignment, profit margin, marketing, markup, price, overhead costs, retail, wholesale and others. The appendix includes more than a dozen useful copier-ready forms that can make pricing and profits easier.

You don't necessarily want to turn your craft into a money machine, but it would be nice to earn some income for your talents and skills while offering quality products to others. By learning to price and sell some of your work you can enjoy your craft even more.

The Crafter's Guide to Pricing Your Work is the first book offering specific pricing information on a wide variety of craft products. It is comprehensive, but it will never be complete. Please share your pricing experiences and ideas with the author by writing to him in care of the publisher so that future editions will be even more helpful to fellow crafters. Write to:

Dan Ramsey, *The Crafter's Guide to Pricing Your Work*
℅ Betterway Books
1507 Dana Avenue
Cincinnati, OH 45207

CHAPTER ONE

The Craft of Pricing Crafts

How much should I charge for my crafts?

This is one of the most commonly asked questions from both new and experienced crafters. And it's a very important question. Though most crafters aren't looking to get rich with their hobby, they do want to pay for materials, buy additional tools, repair current equipment and have something to show for their time and skills.

This chapter introduces you to the craft of pricing. In it you'll learn how *all* products—from bobbins to boats—are priced. You'll also learn how to sell the value of your craft. You'll discover tips on how to negotiate, how to sell to friends, and how and when to raise your prices.

Most important, you'll add a new skill to your toolbox: You'll learn how to give greater value to your craft customers.

Making Money With Your Craft

Maybe one of these situations has happened to you:

- Someone wants to buy your crafts, but you don't know how much to charge.
- You cannot afford to purchase some expensive materials for your next project.
- You cannot justify the cost of repairing your old kiln, but you cannot bear to part with it either.
- You need some additional income and would like to sell some of your crafts.
- Your spouse is pressuring you to spend less time in your craft room and more time in the kitchen or yard.

■ You want to retire soon and would like to develop an income from your craft to cover expenses and offer a profit.

Pricing your work can be one of the most frustrating components of craft—until you understand that pricing is a combination of craft and art. You can learn the craft of pricing just as you developed the crafts of selecting and finishing raw materials. Art comes after years of applying craft until it is second nature.

Helen Frankl enjoyed making quilts. Over the years, Helen's quilts became popular in her community and she sold dozens of them. Even so, Helen figured that she averaged less than three dollars an hour for the labor she put into her quilts. With her husband soon retiring, Helen wanted to make more money from her skills. She didn't want a big business, just a fair income for her time and skills.

Her friend, a business consultant, explained the craft of pricing and showed her how to sell value. Within six months, Helen was selling fewer quilts, but making an average of fourteen dollars an hour for her time, plus paying expenses. With advanced marketing ideas (chapter seven), Helen expects to increase her income even further. Just as important, Helen gets more enjoyment from quilting because she realizes the value of her skills. And so do others.

Why should you consider the craft of pricing? Doesn't art sell itself?

No, it doesn't. Art requires the craft of pricing to enhance its value.

Craftsmanship is applying your knowledge of and "feel" for art to tangible projects. Craftsmanship transforms the natural beauty of minerals into beautiful jewelry. It adds to the attractiveness of natural fibers. It expresses the individuality of the craftsperson and the customer. Craftsmanship brings art to life and gives it function.

The craft of pricing your work is as important as other crafts you use. And, while art sets its own value and sells itself, the craft of marketing must be applied to ensure that those who appreciate fine crafts have the opportunity to purchase it. That's what this book is all about: pricing and marketing your craft.

Understanding Pricing

What is pricing?

You've stopped at a local craft shop for a new glue gun. A low-temperature glue gun with glue sticks has a sign in front of it that says "$1995." Your experience tells you that it certainly isn't one thousand nine hundred and ninety-five dollars. It must be nineteen dollars and ninety-five cents. You think for a moment: "I paid $18 for my last glue gun and it lasted quite awhile. I got a lot of use out of it. I'll get it."

A price is simply what you're willing to give up in exchange for what you want. You would not give up nearly $2,000 for a glue gun, but it is worth about $20 to you. That $20 may have cost you a couple hours of your time but, you figure, the glue gun will save you many times more than that. So you exchange $19.95 (plus tax, of course) in cash for what you want.

This process is repeated at the grocery store, the car lot and anywhere you give someone money for what you want. It's much easier to give the store your money than bring in some of your crafts to exchange. You exchange what you have (time and skills) for what you want (glue gun, groceries, car). Money is a convenient measurement for the exchange. The next customer at the craft store may be exchanging the equivalent of a half hour's time and skills for the glue gun—or six hours' time and skills. In each case, the craft store gets the same amount of money. That's their price.

How did the craft store set the price of the glue gun? The store or the manufacturer probably conducted some "market research" to determine the price at which people will exchange money for the glue gun while allowing a fair profit for both the manufacturer and the store.

Market research is a craft in itself. Basically, though, it answers four questions about pricing:

1. *How much is the glue gun worth to the customer?* That is, what is the value of the benefit that the glue gun gives to someone who buys it? If it saves the customer time, how much time? How much is that time worth to the typical customer?

2. *What will customers actually pay for a glue gun?* This question considers the customer's experience in buying glue guns. Are glue guns on the market priced above $50? Below $10? Or in the range of $15 to $40?

3. *Can the manufacturer and retailer pay for costs and make a profit at that price?* This is an important question. If the retailer cannot sell glue guns at more than $10, the price he must pay for them, he cannot pay for the cost of operating his store and will lose money on each sale.

4. *Can the retailer make more profit by selling a few glue guns at a higher price or more at a lower price?* You see the answer to this question everywhere. Fancy craft stores sell a few specialized glue guns at higher prices while the

discount stores sell hundreds of basic glue guns at lower prices. Both profit because there are people who shop for price alone while others shop for value.

Of course, you can't be like the woman who had a sign on her teddy bears that read. "$1,000 each." When asked if she sold any she said, "Not yet. But when I do, I'm going to make a *big* profit!"

Pricing Types

Pricing glue guns, or groceries, or automobiles is a complex process that requires the investment of hundreds of hours and many thousands of dollars. Pricing your crafts is much easier, yet it applies many of the same rules and techniques.

Simplified Pricing

Most new crafters use the simplified pricing system. They multiply the number of hours required to complete the job by a basic hourly rate, then add in the materials. For example, a leather purse may take three hours to tool. The crafter multiplies three hours by, say, $10 an hour, then adds in $15 for the cost of materials. The total comes to $45. That's the price.

There are many problems with this method of pricing. First, it doesn't pay you enough for your skills and your tools. Once you've deducted the cost of tool replacement, books and classes, services and utilities, you're getting minimum wage. And you're still not earning any interest on the money you've invested in your tools and equipment.

Sophisticated Pricing

Let's look at how many successful businesses price their products and services.

The first step to pricing your craft is determining what type of price to set. Are you pricing neck jewelry that you will sell at craft shows (retail) or to a jewelry store (wholesale)? If you are wholesaling your products, at what price do you suggest the retailer sell them?

A *retailer* sells a product to the ultimate or final consumer. The retail price is the price at which the product is sold to the consumer. A *wholesaler* buys the product from a manufacturer and sells it to the retailer at the wholesale price. A *manufacturer* makes the product and sells it to the wholesaler, the retailer or directly to the consumer.

To set the price of your craft you need information about the cost of materials, the time required to make the piece (labor), the cost of "overhead," and the amount of profit you should reasonably expect. Let's look at each of these components in brief.

MATERIAL COST

Material cost is the cost of the materials used directly in the final product, such as clay and glaze for ceramics. Supplies such as brushes are part of overhead, and not material cost. However, the cost of picking up materials or having them shipped to you is a part of the cost of the materials rather than overhead.

LABOR COST

Labor cost is the cost of work directly applied to manufacturing the craft product. Labor not directly applied to making the product is an overhead cost. Labor cost includes both the hourly wage and the cost of any fringe benefits.

OVERHEAD COST

Overhead cost includes all costs other than direct material costs and direct labor. Overhead is the indirect cost of making your craft product. For example, the cost of a studio and clean-up time are overhead costs. Think of material and labor as direct costs—expenses that can be directly tied to the making of a specific craft product—and overhead as indirect costs that cannot be charged to a specific product. If you have purchased this book to make a profit with your craft—which I assume you have—the cost of the book is an indirect cost you can deduct from your taxes as a legitimate business expense. It is a part of your overhead.

PROFIT

Profit is the amount of money you have left over once you've paid all the bills. Many crafters who have invested hundreds or even thousands of dollars into their equipment and skills never consider that they should receive a return on that investment. They would never think of renting money to a bank interest free, but will to their business. A fair profit is vital to the success of your craft enterprise. Without it, your craft business may not be here a year from now to serve new customers.

In addition, you may have different costs for different crafts you do. The direct and indirect (overhead) costs for making lace are less than for forging metals. So you should calculate the costs separately.

Using Markup

One popular method of pricing crafts is called markup. Markup is a percentage of the materials cost that is added to cover labor and operating expenses. For example, a cake decorator may add 300 percent of the cost of materials as the cost of labor, another 100 percent for the cost of equipment (oven, pans, supplies, etc.) and another 100 percent for profit. That's a total markup of 500 percent, or 5 times the materials cost. If the materials for a wedding cake cost $15, the markup is $75 ($15 × 5) and the total price is $90 ($15 + $75).

Does that mean the profit on this job is 100 percent? Not at all. It is actually $15 (100 percent × the materials cost of $15) or about 16.66 percent of the total price of $90. The profit is then just over 16 percent. Profit will be covered in more detail later in this chapter.

Another way of looking at markup pricing is to establish a "rule of thumb." In the above example, the rule of thumb is to price the job at 6 times the materials cost (100 percent of materials cost + 500 percent for markup = 600 percent or 6 ×).

Estimating Material Costs

As noted earlier, your material cost is the price you paid for any materials that are used in making your craft project. For ceramics, it is the clay and glazes. It is also the cost of getting the materials to your studio, such as shipping charges or car mileage charges to pick it up. However, material costs do not include the cost of your brushes, kiln or related studio costs. These are considered overhead.

Recordkeeping

How can you know how much a specific material costs? The large block of clay you purchased may have been cut up into smaller pieces. The answer is to keep good records. The appendix of this book includes a sample Materials Purchase Record and a sample Materials Use Record. They give you a place to record the actual costs of materials that you purchase and how you use them in your craft. You don't have to account for every component of your craft, but by keeping track of how you use your materials you will soon learn how much it costs—and be better able to price your craft.

As an example, suppose you produce animal figures from sculpturing compound. You buy two pounds of compound for $10. Shipping is another $3.50, so the total is $13.50 for two pounds or 32 ounces. If each of your figures requires 4 ounces of compound, you can sculpt eight figures from the two-pound package (32 divided by 4). Divide $13.50 (materials cost) by 8 (units per package) and you have a cost of $1.69 per figure.

This same principle can be applied to any type of craft. As you buy a block of sculpturing compound you record the total material cost, figure its cost by ounce or pound, and keep track of its use. By keeping these records you can accurately estimate the cost of materials for a job in just a few minutes.

In some cases, costing materials can be more work than it is worth. For instance, you won't want to count each spot of glue and add $0.001 for each one you use. Instead, you can estimate the number of units you will use on a "typical" project, figure the approximate cost of glue for the project and record it in your pricing book. So, in estimating a future project, you add in that figure for glue. As your craft business grows and you spend hundreds of dollars on adhesives you can review your costs. But for now, a rough estimate will be sufficient. Yes, dimes make dollars but pennies can be ignored until they add up to dimes.

Pricing Book

This is a good time to start your pricing book. It will be a place to record what you're learning about pricing your craft. It can be a loose-leaf three-ring binder, a bound "Record" book, a card file, a manila folder or a file on your computer. In it you can include material worksheets, labor and

CRAFTER'S GUIDE TO PRICING YOUR WORK

overhead worksheets, estimate worksheets, and any rules of thumb that you develop.

One more point: Although you may consider keeping all these records a waste of time, it's not. In fact, by learning how to price your craft through good records you'll reduce the time it takes to develop an accurate price. You'll also reduce the time you spend on unprofitable craft projects. You'll have more time for doing what you enjoy—and what makes you money.

Estimating Labor Costs

No two crafters work in the same way or at the same speed. One may insist on only using hand tools. Another will build with the latest power tool using jigs for mass production. Skill levels and experience will also differ. Even so, accurate labor costs can be set by learning how *you* work.

The appendix of this book includes a typical Time Sheet for crafters. It offers an easy way to record the amount of time needed to do a specific project. The time sheet can be used chronologically, writing down the task description and time it took in the order in which it was done. Or you can keep track of your time on a chronological time sheet and then summarize time by task on a labor worksheet.

Using Worksheets

How you track your time depends on the type of tasks you perform, how long they take, and how you feel about writing everything down. You certainly don't want to spend more time recording your activities than it takes to do them. Tasks can be summarized, such as: assembled frame for 8″ × 10″ drawing: 0.5 hours.

What should you include on your labor worksheets? Record any activities that are directly related to craft production such as time needed to design the project, set up equipment, gather materials, produce and clean up for that project. You can also record cleanup time for estimating overhead, but then don't include it in your project labor worksheet figures.

Labor costs are more than the hourly wage you pay yourself and/or your workers. Labor costs must also include employment taxes, health or retirement benefits, the cost of required work clothing and related expenses.

Remember, if you are the sole employee, pay yourself at least as much as you would pay an employee with your skills.

Your Time and Your Skills

What are you selling when you sell your labor? It's more than just your time. You're also selling your creativity, your originality, your knowledge and your skills. If you are producing a one-of-a-kind work of art, your creativity, originality, knowledge and skills are extensive and you may earn thousands of dollars for your product. If you are making teddy bears, you will be paid for your creativity and your skills, but not your originality because you are copying someone else's creative design. If you are mass-producing decoupage plaques, your skills are high but creativity and originality are probably not—and you will be paid accordingly for your labor.

Remember that estimating labor for your time and skills requires efficient use of both. A basket that you weave over a weekend doesn't require two days to build. When estimating actual working time, estimate how much time it would take to build the product if you were doing it all day every day. That same basket may take only two and a half hours of actual production time. By reducing production time you can increase your hourly labor rate. In fact, one of the keys to making more money as a crafter is using your knowledge and experience to increase your productivity. The more you can do in an hour, the more you make per hour.

Estimating Overhead Costs

Overhead costs are all costs other than direct materials and direct labor. Overhead is the indirect cost of making your craft product. Overhead costs include rent (or a portion of the cost of your home), tools, electricity, telephone, taxes and "miscellaneous" expenses.

The appendix of this book includes a form for estimating your overhead expenses. You can either make entries directly on this worksheet or transfer them from other records you keep. Let's look at each overhead cost individually.

Rent

If you are renting a studio for your craft, this is an easy calculation. You simply enter the amount of your monthly rent and any related costs. However, most hobby crafters start in their garage or a room of their home. Can you deduct some costs of your home if you use a portion of it to make money? Yes! Call the Internal Revenue Service Forms Hotline at (800) 829-3676 and ask them to send you *Business Use of Your Home* (Publication 587). It will help you determine whether you can deduct part of your home as a business and list the expenses you can include. I'll list other valuable tax publications you can get for free in chapter seven.

Tools

Tools are a vital part of your craft. You can't create without them. They are a cost of production. So they are a legitimate expense as you begin selling your craft. A $1,200 loom is an overhead expense if you use it to make a profit with your craft.

As you purchase more expensive tools, you can either "expense" or "depreciate" them for tax purposes. To expense a tool, you simply include the entire cost as an expense during the year you buy the tool. (Refer to IRS Section 179.) The cost of a $1,200 loom can be a deductible expense for that year even though you may use it for four years. If you depreciate the same loom over the four years, you can deduct $300 a year as an expense. Depreciation, however, should be left up to accountants as there are many ways to depreciate tools and equipment. Once your small craft business has grown, you can talk to an accountant about this opportunity.

Whether you expense or depreciate your tools at tax time, you need to calculate their approximate cost so you know how much to charge for overhead. If you expect to use your new $900 sewing machine for three years, then sell it for $300, the sewing machine costs you about $16.67 per month—plus the cost of maintenance and repairs.

List all of your tools and their current value on the worksheet in the appendix. Group tools as needed: 28 acrylic paintbrushes = $200. Include an estimate of their expected life before you will need to replace them. Depending on use, some tools will be upgraded every year while others can be replaced every ten years.

Utilities

Utilities are next. Estimate the cost of electricity, telephone and other utility expenses on a monthly basis. If you are using your personal telephone to make business calls, you can only deduct the cost of long distance calls and other services needed for your business. However, if you have installed a second phone or a second line into your craft studio or work area, include the cost as part of your overhead expenses.

Taxes

Taxes are a part of your overhead expenses. You will have to pay income tax on any supplemental income from your craft (less expenses). In fact, if you start making serious money with your craft, the federal and many state governments will require you to make estimated tax payments every three months. The free IRS booklets listed in chapter seven will get you started. For most hobby crafters, the amount of taxes they pay is minimal. Some simply have their full-time employer take out an extra $50 or $100 a month to cover possible tax liability from their part-time craft business.

Make sure you find out if crafters in your area are required to charge sales tax on retail sales of crafts. If so, call your state revenue office to determine how and when to do so. While state sales taxes are not a cost of doing business for you, their collection can add to your costs. This is not a requirement if you sell all of your products wholesale to retailers, but you may be responsible for an inventory tax. (An Inventory Record form is included in the appendix of this book.) Check with state and local governments.

Estimating Profits

How much profit should you expect to make as you sell your craft projects? The simplest answer is you should receive a return on your investment equal to what you would receive if you invested it somewhere else with equal risk. That is, if all of your tools and studio are worth about $2,000, what interest would you earn if you invested that money in someone else's craft business? The answer is typically between 10 and 20 percent. That's the return on investment you should expect from investing in your operation.

What is profit? It's the money that remains from your sales after you've paid your expenses. It's figured like this:

Sales – Total Costs = Profit

If you sell $10,000 worth of craft products that cost you $9,000 to make, your profit is $1,000. But it's not quite that simple. Your wages as a crafter/business owner/manager should be considered part of the total costs, but the tax man considers your wages to be part of your profits. For the purpose of figuring how to price your craft, though, consider your wages as part of total costs and think of profit as your reward for being daring enough to be your own boss.

One successful crafter keeps track of her income, expenses and profit on a computer using a spreadsheet program. Once a month she makes all entries and determines whether her business is making a profit. If the profit is lower than her goal she reduces expenses as appropriate. She may hold off purchasing a special tool or stocking up on materials, or she may reduce her own wages for the month to ensure that her profit goal is reached.

Setting Your Studio Rate

Why do you need to keep such close track of your time and expenses? Because you are going to be paid for them. Once you've developed a "studio rate" you will multiply it by the time it takes to perform the task to determine the labor costs. As an example, you will multiply a studio rate of $32 times the 0.5 hour it took to assemble a frame to come up with a labor cost of $16.

A crafter's studio rate is the cost of labor plus overhead plus profit. As a formula:

Labor + Overhead + Profit = Studio Rate.

Notice that your studio rate is not the same as your hourly wage for labor.

Now the big question: what should your studio rate be? Most professional craft studios charge $25 to $65 an hour. Chapters two through six will offer typical studio rates for specific crafts.

Materials

+

Studio Rate

(Labor + Overhead + Profit)

+

Sales Costs

=

Price

Your studio rate is your number for calculating costs and setting prices.

As an example, a skilled crafter feels he would have to pay $15 an hour to hire himself. He then adds the cost of a benefits package (one-third, or $5 per hour) for a total labor cost of $20 per hour. Overhead comes to $5 per hour to cover studio rent (his garage), tools, utilities and basic supplies. The total is now up to $25. He wants a profit of 10 percent on the total which equals $2.50 per hour. The total is now $27.50. He rounds it off to $28 and sets that amount as his "posted" studio rate.

To set a fair studio rate, consider the caliber of skill and the cost of the tools needed to make your craft. As a guideline, the studio rate for a craft that requires few skill is typically $25 to $35 an hour, depending on the value of tools required. The studio rate for moderately advanced skills is typically $35 to $45 an hour. An artisan with specialized skills which are in high demand charges $55 to $65 an hour. If you're just learning your trade and don't feel comfortable charging these rates, start off as a trainee with a studio rate of $15 to $25 an hour. In each case, the lower rate within the skill category is for crafts that require few tools and the high end is for crafts with expensive tools.

Remember that your studio rate is your number for calculating costs and setting pricing. In most cases, you won't tell your customers what your studio rate is. They don't know what it involves and cannot compare your studio rate to anyone's but their own—which you usually don't want them to do.

Here's how it all comes together. By keeping good records, you've determined that you can produce and finish six identical hand puppets in about three hours, materials cost around $20, and overhead (tools, utilities, taxes, etc.) and profit are built into your studio rate of $30 an hour. So you estimate that six puppets can profitably be built for $110 (three hours at $30/hour + $20 for materials). That's $18.33 per puppet. You might then price them at $18.95 each, or $19.95 for the first with each additional one at $17.95. You may decide to price red puppets at $17.95 and multicolored ones at $19.95. Or, you can look at what competitors are getting for their puppets and price yours at $24.95 each.

Here's a warning from many successful crafters I interviewed: Pricing your products to beat the competition is a good idea, but make sure it's a price that also covers your costs. If it doesn't, find a product where there is less competition and a better opportunity for you to earn a profit at what you enjoy doing.

Maybe you already have established a studio rate that is lower than that of most professional craft studios. How can you increase your studio rate to this level? First, make sure you are working as efficiently as possible. Chapter seven will include a number of proven ideas on how to make your crafting more efficient. The key to a higher studio rate is higher efficiency. Second, once you've established your new studio rate, set a date when it will become effective and let your prospects and customers know. It will give you more business now—as prospects order before the price increase— and will give you more profit later as your studio rate goes up.

Odd Pricing

Let's talk about "odd pricing." Odd pricing is setting a price that is just under a whole dollar amount. Instead of $30, an odd-priced item is $29.99, $29.95, etc. Odd pricing was begun many years ago to give the illusion of a lower or bargain price. It is so widely used in pricing everything from crackers to cars that many people round it off in their heads: "about thirty bucks."

Should a crafter use odd pricing? Much depends on what you're selling and for how much. If you are selling inexpensive craft products that the consumer can purchase from other sources, consider using odd pricing, especially for items under $10. However, for most craft products, prices should be rounded up to the nearest $.50 for items under $10, the nearest $1 between $11 and $50, the nearest $5 between $51 and $100, the nearest $10 between $100 and $250, and the nearest $50 above $250. For example, if you decide that the retail price should be about $114, round it up to $120.

YECH Pricing

One popular method of pricing a product or service—one that can easily be applied to pricing your craft—is called YECH (rhymes with "etch") pricing. YECH is an acronym that stands for:

You
Economy
Competition
Hunger

Your Costs

Here's how it works. First, you add all of the direct and indirect costs required to make and sell your craft product. You estimate direct materials costs, set your labor costs, define indirect or overhead costs, establish your profit margin, just as illustrated before.

The Economy

Second, you consider the economy in the area where your craft products will sell. Is the economy growing and do customers have money for discretionary spending? Or is unemployment high and do people have little money for fine crafts? If your economy is not strong, consider selling your craft products in a region that is, or in a nearby community where people with higher incomes live and purchase. What is the economic makeup of your prospective customers? Are they conditioned to expect high price tags that allow you to invest more time in your products? Or are they looking for something that will do the job at the lowest cost?

The Competition

Third, always look at what your competition is selling and the price they are getting. Your competition is not limited to individuals selling items exactly like yours, it is everyone who competes for the same dollar. That is, if you make baskets, other crafters who are making decorative crafts are your competitors. They're going after the same dollar that you are. How are they doing? What are they selling? For how much? In your experienced opinion, what are their direct and indirect costs? How can you compete with them and still make a profit?

Hunger

Finally, pricing is controlled by hunger. Your hunger. All of your calculations of indirect costs (overhead) are based on a specific amount of sales. If your overhead costs are $200 a month and you expect to make twenty units in a month, the indirect costs are $10 per unit—if you sell twenty. But if you sell just one unit that month, the indirect costs for that single unit are the full $200. So you may decide to sell a few units more at a discount in order to recoup part of your overhead. Or you may be hungry to make a sale to a specific client and decide to discount a piece to do so.

Here's the other side of hunger: You're full. You have enough work to keep you busy for the foreseeable future, but one customer insists that they must have one of your craft projects by the end of next week. So you price the project at a premium. You are paying yourself overtime.

Problem Projects

One more point: There will be some projects or some people that you know will become a problem. The project will require additional time to search for matching stock or the customer is a grumbler who will not be satisfied until they've returned it to you three times. Many professional workers add what I call a PITA fee to these types of projects. PITA is an acronym for "pain in the anterior." You get the picture. The trick is determining which projects should include this "fee" in the pricing. Some crafters figure about 5 percent of their projects will include difficult tasks or people and add this into their studio rate. Experience will guide you.

Price vs. Volume

In establishing your pricing, you have estimated the volume or amount of sales you expect to make. There are two sides to the price-vs.-volume issue. Should you go for higher prices and lower volume, or should you try to sell more with a lower price. There is no correct answer that fits everyone. Much depends on YECH:

You: Do you prefer to sell a few or many?

Economy: Does your market prefer lower price or higher quality?

Competition: Does your competition sell price or quality?

Hunger: Which will best help you pay your expenses?

For example, a sculptor preferred to produce unique fountain statues for luxury homes in her area, but the economy changed and such homes weren't being built. She learned that many homeowners were remodeling their homes to look like finer homes. So, temporarily, she mass-produced smaller statues for homeowners and remodelers. In fact, she used the reputation she had built as a fine sculptor to help sell these more reasonably priced statues. Her answer to the price-vs.-volume questions is: Follow the needs of the market.

Sell Value Over Price

"What we obtain too cheap, we esteem too lightly."—Thomas Paine

Thus far, the emphasis has been on learning your exact production cost before setting the price of your craft. This method ensures that you will cover your actual expenses and make a reasonable return on your investment and skills. However, your best opportunities for profitability are to sell on value rather than on price.

People who buy crafts don't want something that looks like it came from a discount store. More and more consumers want products that have their own personality—and are willing to pay for it. They want value!

What a decorative necklace cost you to make is really irrelevant to the buyer. The real issue is: What is the necklace worth to the buyer? How much money will this buyer give you in exchange for the benefits that this necklace gives him or her. The answer depends on how many of the benefits the buyer can see and value. It's your job as an artisan to help the buyer see the value of your craft product.

The buyer can go to a department store and buy a necklace. That's utility value. In this case, utility value may be $5. Or the buyer can find a mass-produced decorative necklace with minimal artistic value for $20. That's the craft value. Or the buyer can purchase your handcrafted necklace made from rare shells, hand selected and skillfully sewn to ensure strength and beauty for $100. That's the artistic value. Why should the buyer purchase your necklace at twenty times the cost of the utility necklace? Because they understand and value the difference between the two.

Sell Artistic Value

To sell the artistic value of your craft product, you must first understand its utility value and its craft value because you are competing with other products on both levels. As an example, if you make high-quality kitchen cutlery, you should know the price a customer will have to pay for plastic-handled kitchen knives that serve the same function. You should also know how much a customer will pay for mass-produced decorative knives. These knives are your competition. By knowing these prices you can help the customer understand the value they will receive by paying more for your quality cutlery.

Copyright Your Work

One proven way to sell value over price is to copyright your work. Besides the obvious protection a copyright gives you as a creative crafter, it also tells your customers that your products are special. A copyright gives the creator/designer the exclusive right to control how, where and when the design is used. This includes reproducing, selling, distributing and displaying the work. These rights belong to the creator during his or her lifetime plus fifty years.

An idea cannot be copyrighted, but the execution of an idea can be. So a wooden chest cannot be copyrighted, but its unique shape or design can be. That's called "artistic craftsmanship."

You can copyright your work by simply putting a copyright notice on the work:

Copyright, 1997, CustomCrafts, Inc.

To register the copyright, write to the U.S. Copyright Office, Library of Congress, Washington, DC 20559 for the required forms and current fee. Ask for Form VA (for registering visual arts).

The Importance of Price

Most crafters who shop for new equipment attempt to balance two factors: price and value. Few people buy on price alone. Before selecting a pottery wheel, for example, the typical potter considers the features and translates them into benefits. A variable speed control on the pottery wheel is a feature. Having a wheel that allows the potter to quickly change speed to match conditions is a benefit. If the benefit makes the crafter's job easier, faster or more profitable, it is a useful benefit that has value.

A specific brand of tool or materials may also have a valued benefit. You may select one brand of pottery wheel over another because your experience—and advertising messages—tells you that owning that brand gives you efficiency, prestige, quality or peace of mind.

As a customer for a new tool, you will ask the price to decide whether the two factors—price and value—are equal. When offering the price, the catalog copy or the salesperson will tell you about the features and benefits of this tool so you can determine value for yourself. Or the salesperson may ask you about your specific needs, then help you define the tool's value in regard to those needs. But you must make the final decision because you are the customer.

How about *your* customers? How can you illustrate the value of your craft product to them? The answer depends on the features and benefits that your product offers to customers. If you are making and selling flower vases, you can display them on a small decorative table with a fine table cloth and beautiful flowers. You can cut a vase in half to show that it is made of quality materials. You can display the set next to a list of its features and benefits:

- quality craftsmanship (feature) for long, useful life (benefit)
- hand-thrown clays (feature) to add beauty to your flower arrangement (benefit)
- durable finish (feature) stands up to daily use (benefit)

You get the picture. In order to sell the value of your craft product, you must make sure the customer knows the product's features and benefits in their own terms.

The appendix of this book includes a worksheet for developing a list of features and benefits for your craft products.

Selling the Value of Your Work

Customers will always want to know the price of your work. That's their nature. You, as a craftsperson, want to make sure they understand the value of your work as well so they can make an informed decision about purchasing it. Depending on what you make and how you sell it, there are many ways you can ensure that your customers know the value of your products as they make that decision.

One successful doll maker knew that most customers who pick up a doll at her craft booth will turn it over to look for a price sticker on the bottom. So she placed stickers on all of her dolls that said, "Great value! Ask me the price." After reading the sticker, most customers would look up to see the craftsperson. Knowing this, she would watch anyone who picked up one of her dolls and try to be ready with eye contact and a smile when they looked up. She would then "break the ice" with a comment like: "That's a beautiful doll." In most cases, the customer would then ask the price and the craftsperson would respond with more comments about its value: "I hand-painted the face to show the innocence of a child" or "I made the outfit just like kids wore when we were young." The craftsperson wanted the customer to set a dollar value in his or her mind before telling the price. She found that, in most cases, the customer would value the piece at or above her actual price. The craftsperson didn't make a sale every time, but her sales increased because she sold value before she told price.

Should You Use Price Tags?

Should you mark your crafts with a price? Much depends on what you sell, to whom and when. Craft products under about $100 are typically priced; items above that amount may be if the prospective buyers are price shoppers. If they are upscale buyers such as in a gallery, pricing often does not need to appear on the item.

If you change the price, should you write over the old price on the sticker? In most cases, no—especially if you have increased the price. Unless your craft is facing tough pricing competition, you should remove the old sticker and put a new sticker on the item with the new price. You should also periodically replace any price stickers that look worn or faded. You don't want customers to think you haven't been able to sell the product since the Ice Age.

Salesmanship

A word about "selling." A craftsperson doesn't actually sell his or her craft product. The craftsperson helps potential customers learn why they will benefit from buying the product. Simply talking with people about what you do, why and how it will benefit them is the best form of salesmanship. The more you talk honestly to people about their needs and your solutions, the more you will sell. No magic formulas or passwords are necessary. Knowledge and sincerity are still the best sales tools. Of course, don't talk politics, religion or anything controversial with customers.

Finally, never wait for the customer to say, "I'll take it." Whenever the customer has shown an interest in your craft by asking a specific question or by commenting on your work, close the sale with a comment or question that helps the customer commit to their internal decision. "Thank you. Can I gift wrap it for you?" Or "Yes, I sanded and finished it by hand. Would you like to have one?" Or "I'm very proud of that piece. Would you prefer the gloss or matte finish?"

Selling Craftsmanship

You can add value to your craft products—and command a higher price—by making each of your products unique. A craft product is typically one copy of a distinct design. There are other copies out there and the customer knows it. A piece of art is singular in itself.

You may make silver rings from a specific design, each one nearly identical to all of the other rings. If you set them out on a table, a customer would think they are all the same—and pay you accordingly. But if you add something artful to each one, they are now original and are worth more to the customer and to you.

How can you make each of your craft products original without pricing yourself out of the market with extra labor costs? If you are making silver rings, produce some settings by hand rather than by machine. Hand-carve a setting, set each ring with a stone of a slightly different color or size, offer to engrave the ring at no additional charge, or number each of your rings as painters number their paintings: 12 of 50.

The more you specialize your craft products, the more they become art rather than craft. You can distinguish your wooden picture frames by hand carving part of the trim design. You can add hand-painted trim or ribbons to baskets. Etching your name in the base of stoneware personalizes each piece. Even selecting exotic materials with varying patterns can give the product an individual and artistic quality.

By adding artistic elements to your craft you are also developing your artistic skills. Then, as your skills grow, you can command an even higher price as you produce truly one-of-a-kind pieces for discriminating customers.

Selling to Friends, Relatives and Neighbors

Chances are, your first customers will be friends, relatives and neighbors. And they're going to want a "deal." How much do you charge your best friend for those oil paintings that take so long to make? What if your neighbor asks you to design gold jewelry for an upcoming anniversary—as long as it's under $25? What if a friend of a friend wants a discount on your stoneware?

The best way to avoid problems and hurt feelings is to have a pricing policy and stick to it. That is, you decide in advance how much of your craft you give away as gifts, how much you will discount any of your works and under what conditions.

As an example, one successful crafter decided that he could not afford to give any of his silver charm bracelets as gifts. Instead, he made a specific number of simple charms during his slow season each year and gave them out as gifts through the coming year. When they were gone, they were gone. He did, however, offer discounts to friends and relatives (20 percent) and acquaintances (10 percent)—if they promised to tell others about his work but not to tell anyone the amount of the discount they received. He considered this a sales commission as these people would become his sales staff and tell others about his work. He didn't give away his work. Nor did he give away the discount. He traded the discount for something of value: word-of-mouth advertising.

What do you say to friends and relatives who ask for free products? You're going to tell them no, but you need to do it in a way that will strengthen your relationship. You can say: "I'm really glad you like my work. I've spent many years developing my skills and many dollars on my tools. And I only use the best materials I can find. I'm sure you understand that

I can't just give them away. But I value our relationship. Let me do this: I'll give you a full 20 percent (or 10 percent) discount on anything I make if you'll tell others about my work. And, of course, you can't tell anyone I've given you a special deal. That takes all of my profit, but I'm willing to do it for you."

If the friend, relative or neighbor still insists on a better price, talk to them about value. Tell them why your craft product is valuable to them. Mention the features and how they will benefit them. Sell them on value. If that still doesn't work, you can either give your time, skills and materials away or you can say "I'm sorry, but no."

Showing Your Crafts

Successful crafters know not only how to price their work, but also how to show it so customers can see its value. Depending on what you're making, the area of the country and how you feel about salesmanship, you have many options for showing your products.

Smaller items, such as jewelry, ceramics and dolls, can easily be shown with a sample. When prospective customers ask about your product you have a sample that you can hand them to examine as you point out its features and benefits.

Use Photos for Larger Items

Larger items, such as sculptures, wedding cakes and dollhouses, are somewhat harder to show. In this case, the best sales tool is photos of completed crafts. If you're handy with a camera you can take these photos yourself. Otherwise you may want to have a professional or at least more experienced photographer take photos of your crafts.

Place your photos in a quality three-ring binder or presentation binder. A presentation binder, available at larger stationery stores, allows you to stand the binder up on its edge for display. Include some sample literature, your business cards and letters from happy customers. Of course, also include any awards, competitions, commissions, reviews and professional credentials that underscore your acceptance as an artisan. You'll have a presentation kit that will help you sell your craft at a fair price.

Even if you show your projects with photos, make sure you have something that the customer can touch and hold such as a sample, a component or even a miniature of the final product. Also, give your prospective customers something to select from, but don't overload them with 31 flavors.

Promoting Your Crafts

Depending on your craft product, you can show your product or pictures in person, in a catalog or in a brochure. Even if you have a sample to show people, you may want a brochure that describes your services, your products and your attitude toward your work. Many printshops have the capability to turn your ideas and photos into a simple brochure. You can give the finished brochure to people at craft shows, friends and relatives, and other artisans. You can mail the brochures to prospective customers and sales representatives, or pass them out at the shopping mall. They make an inexpensive and practical way of telling others about your craft and how they will benefit from calling you.

One successful crafter sold her embroidery at craft fairs. She had a giveaway drawing at each event for an impressive, but easy-to-make, piece. Those who signed up for the drawing were sent a brochure, price sheet and order form for her other embroidery crafts.

There are many other ways to inexpensively promote your craft venture. While brochures are one of the best, business cards also work very well. A local printer, copy shop or desktop publishing shop can help you design and write effective business cards. They can be given to friends, relatives and acquaintances, tacked up on local bulletin boards or traded with noncompeting craftspeople. If you have a particularly photogenic product, you can have its picture taken and used as the background of your business card.

Other successful craft businesses have postcards printed up with pictures of their products on the back side and information about their business on the left half of the front. These cards can serve as business cards, brochures and mailing pieces. Be creative in your marketing as well as in your craft.

Striving for Quality

Quality is the characteristic of excellence; it means a product is the best it can be under the circumstances. A quality hand-woven rug is made of the best fabrics available for the money spent, designed with knowledgeable craftsmanship and given careful consideration to detail. Quality is *not* perfection. It is what it should be: functional and aesthetic.

Most crafters strive for excellence. They want to apply their skills and their self to making functional and beautiful things from quality materials. They understand that building a reputation for quality can somewhat limit the business they do, but it is worth the effort.

However, being a quality crafter doesn't necessarily mean that others will see the quality that is put into each job. What should you do? Should you lower your standard? Should you maintain quality and price yourself out of the market? These are tough questions that every professional crafter must answer.

Set Your Own Standards

Some crafters decide that spending additional hours in details that the customers will not see or appreciate is part of their standard of quality. Others feel that it is not true quality if it does not directly benefit the customer. In fact, they contend that unrecognized quality prices an otherwise valuable product out of the hands of all but a few buyers. They would rather reach more buyers with good quality than only a few buyers with perfection. Some crafters disagree and feel that quality requires coming as close to perfection as possible.

Which viewpoint is correct? Both and neither. Quality is not an absolute, but a standard. You establish your own standard for the work you do and, in order to sell your craft, that standard must meet the standard established by the buyer. If it exceeds the buyer's standard it will also probably exceed his or her ability to pay.

Once you've decided what standard of quality works best for you and your prospective customers, you can decide how best to build your reputation for quality. You may want to develop a reputation for using only the most unusual materials, for creative designs or for using natural materials in new ways. (You certainly don't want to develop a reputation for doing all things with all materials.)

How do you promote your standard of quality? You do so by the work you do. But you can also build your reputation for quality by simply defining your attitude toward your work and making sure that others know what it is. You can choose a slogan that clearly reflects your attitudes toward quality:

Enhancing the beauty of gold and silver.
Designing lace to be enjoyed by future generations.
Memorable wedding cakes for memorable weddings.
Teddy bears to cherish forever.
Silhouettes that capture your spirit.

Your attitude toward workmanship becomes the slogan for your craft business. It tells others what you do and why you do it. Use this slogan on your business cards and literature. Have it reproduced on small labels with your name and address, and attach the labels to every piece you make. It will help you develop your reputation for quality. It will also help you sell your craft at a fair price.

Using a Business Name

One proven method of developing a reputation for quality is giving your craft venture a quality name. For example, an enterprising crafter in Des Moines, Iowa, named his business Creative Looms. It gave customers an image of a large firm that featured artistic designs. Customers didn't know that his studio was a spare bedroom and he was the entire work force. The image worked and his business eventually outgrew the bedroom because he named his business for the size he wanted it to be rather than what it was.

An assumed business name is a name other than the real and true name of each person operating a business. A real and true name becomes an assumed business name with the addition of any words that imply the existence of additional owners. For example, "Nancy Jones" is a real and true name, while "Nancy Jones Company" is an assumed business name.

In most states and counties, you must register an assumed business name to let the public know who is transacting business under that name. Without the registration you may be fined; even worse, you may not be able to defend a legal action because your assumed business name wasn't properly registered.

In many states, an assumed business name is registered with the state's corporate division. Some states will also register your assumed business name with counties in which you do business. Other states require that you do so. In some locations, you must publish a public notice in an area newspaper stating that you (and any other business principals) are operating under a specific business name.

In some communities, you may also need a local business license. The best way to learn what requirements are for your area is to contact your state government. Some states have a "one-stop" business telephone number where you can find out what the requirements are, or at least the phone numbers of governing offices.

Additional information on the business side of your craft is offered in chapter seven of this book as well as in Kathryn Caputo's book, *How to Start Making Money with Your Craft* (Betterway Books). Another excellent resource for the business side of crafts is Barbara Brabec's popular *Homemade Money* (Betterway Books).

Negotiating for Fun and Profit

How do you keep from giving away your time and talents to people who feel it necessary to negotiate your price—no matter what it is?

The first step is to know the price you must get for your product. You've learned this price by determining the time it takes to make your product, setting a value for your time, knowing the cost of materials, and establishing the amount of profit you need to earn. You know, for example, you must get at least $35 for your ceramic vases in order to cover materials and labor costs and to make a minimum return on your investment.

Giving the Customers a "Deal"

From this point, you can price your products to take into account the fact that some people will not buy from you unless they can get a "deal." It's not the amount, but the fact that they got it for less than other people pay. It's a matter of pride with them. If you're selling at craft shows, there will be a higher percentage of people who want to deal than if you are selling wholesale to gift shops. You price accordingly. You sell the vases to craft stores at $35 each and you price them at craft shows at $50 each to cover show costs and allow for negotiation.

Remember, the "H" in YECH pricing stands for "hunger." If the show is ready to close and you don't want to take your products home with you, you may decide to offer a discount to any amount above your cost.

Actually, negotiating can be fun. In fact, some crafters look forward to craft shows when they can "deal" with customers face to face. Once you know your minimum price, you can make it a game. As long as you get your minimum price, you win and the customer wins. How much you win depends on your skills as a negotiator.

Negotiation Tips

Here are some techniques that negotiators use to make deals that are win-win situations.

What you give away has no value. If you automatically give a 10 percent discount to customers who blink their eyes twice, they feel that you've inflated your price. Instead, offer to trade value for value. "I'll give you a 10 percent discount on this item if you will write me a letter of recommendation that I can show to prospective customers."

Offer an alternative piece. If a customer wants to offer you $7 for your $10 candle, offer one that is smaller or a display candle that has seen use. Or you can offer less-than-perfect items that are kept under the counter. Label them: Crafts I Did Before My First Cup of Coffee. (More on pricing "seconds" later in this chapter.)

Ask "If I sell it to you for that price, what will you do for me?" Some people will offer to send friends to you or give you something of value. Others won't. What you decide to accept in trade is up to you. The point is that you are showing that the discount you are offering has value.

Here's a technique for tough customers: Ask the customer what they do for a living, then request an equal discount from them. If the customer owns a restaurant, ask for an equal value in meals. If they work in a gas station, are they authorized to trade fuel with you? Whether or not the deal is accepted, the customer realizes that the discount they request has value. You can then suggest a smaller discount or a token trade, or simply give the discount because you want them as a customer. In each case, the customer understands that they have received something of worth and not just a valueless discount.

Another technique is to respond to a low bid by restating it and asking for a higher bid. "Forty-five dollars? Can't you give me a better offer than that?" It doesn't refuse the bid, it just asks for a higher one. Or you can ask in a more friendly way: "Help me. I want to sell you this, but I have to cover my costs. Please make a better offer."

Some crafters will respond to a low bid with points of value until the customer offers what they consider is an acceptable price.

Customer: I'll give you $75.

Crafter: This porcelain plate was hand-painted.

Customer: I'll make it $80.

Crafter: The plate was fired using expensive finishes and a special
process that I learned from a master craftsman.

Customer: $90.

Crafter: Sold!

Sometimes the best response to a ludicrous offer is to ignore it. Another is to use humor. Say with a smile: "I'll give you $2 for that shirt you're wearing!" Humor can diffuse the situation and give you a chance to think of a more appropriate response, such as: "Why?"

Maintaining Your Pricing

"My brother, Harry, bought one of these from you last year for twenty bucks less. I want the same deal!"

How can you maintain your pricing when many people ask for special deals and friend-of-a-friend discounts? The same rule applies: Set your price fairly and stay with it as much as possible. Keep in mind that if you give too many discounts, you'll either lose money or you will have to raise your prices to cover your costs. If you do discount, have a good reason: Competitors are selling it for less and you don't want to lose business to them; you haven't sold enough this month to cover all of your overhead costs; or selling a few more will help you get a better discount from your suppliers.

You can also disarm discount customers by taking their side: "You're right, sir, I did sell one to your brother, Harry, last year for less than my current price. I certainly don't blame you for wanting one at the same price. I will be happy to give you the same price on the same product, but I've added a number of features to it since then and use more expensive materials. It's now worth about $50 more than last year's version. But I'm only charging $20 more." Then go on to explain the additional value.

Remember to apply the first rule of pricing your craft: Sell value over price. Make a habit of answering *any* question about pricing with information about value. Only when your customer understands the value of your craft product should you tell them the price.

Pricing "Seconds"

Of course, crafters don't make mistakes. However, they do sometimes produce "learning experiences" and less-than-perfect products. Can you sell these second-quality products? If so, for how much?

Whether you sell your seconds and to whom depends on who your primary customer is. If your customer is a gallery and your products must represent your best work, don't try to sell them anything less. However, if you are selling your craft products directly to the public at craft shows, you can have an area—above or beneath your display table—set aside for seconds. Identify these less-than-perfect products in some way so that your customers and those who see your products know that this is not your best work. Craftspeople who place their name or a logo on all of their work do not do so on seconds. Others write "imperfect" in an inconspicuous place such as the base or back.

How much should you charge for seconds? Most crafters simply double the price of materials as long as it doesn't exceed about half of the retail price. For example, a doll made from $6 in materials should be priced at about $12 unless the retail price for first quality items is less than $24. If first quality retails for $20, price the second at $10.

Consider two more things when pricing seconds: First, mark the product with the full retail price then show the discounted price. For example, the above doll would be marked "Regular Price: $24; Imperfect Price: $12." Second, make sure that the customer knows that all sales of imperfect products are final. You want the customer to perceive these seconds as of less value than your first quality products, otherwise the customer will feel your products are overpriced.

To close a sale on a second, show the buyer how he or she can make the repair or hide the imperfection. Don't offer to do it for them, no matter how minor.

Some crafters will use their seconds to lure customers to the booth. Others will display seconds in a separate area. Still other craftspeople will keep seconds below the display table, only bringing them out when it looks like a sale will be lost because of price. Your technique for pricing and selling seconds depends on what you're selling, how you're selling and to whom. As you get the opportunity, try each of these techniques to determine which will increase your total sales and profit.

Raising Your Prices

You may now be thinking: "$35 an hour is a lot of money; I'll never be able to get that for my work." In fact, there will soon be a day when you should consider raising your studio rate. When? When your customers tell you to!

How will your customers tell you to raise prices on your craft? By keeping you too busy. As an example, if you find that ten hours a week is all you want to spend on your craft yet you have more than enough business to fill more hours, it's time to raise your prices. Or if you've set aside your Saturdays for profitable crafting and you're booked up for the next three months, increase your studio rate or your time on each project. You have too much business.

Rather than raise prices, some crafters will decide to spend more time at their part-time business. They may even decide to turn it into a full-time venture within a year. But most crafters prefer to make more money for the hours they do work so they can have additional funds for retirement, vacations or special needs.

The 80/20 Rule

A good indicator that it's time to raise prices is when all customers are willing to pay full price for your crafts. The ideal is to follow the 80/20 rule: 80 percent of your prospective customers should be happy with your prices. At least 20 percent of those to whom you give quotes should turn you down for price. Most will do so because your price is too high. Some, though, will do so because your price is too low for the quality they expect.

If only 40 percent of your prospective customers are buying from you, consider lowering your price until you are as busy as you want to be. If it increases to 80 percent, think about increasing your prices.

How Much to Increase

How much of a price increase should you make? Of course, that depends somewhat on what your current price is. If your studio rate is just $20 an hour, you need to get it up to the $30 to $55 an hour range that many professional crafters get. Depending on how busy you are, you may decide to increase rates to $25 an hour now and to $30 an hour in six months if business hasn't dropped off below your desired level. Many crafters increase their studio rate by approximately 5 percent each year just before their busy season. Others do so every 18 months or two years.

Another option is to increase the unit price for your craft product while maintaining your hourly studio rate. That is, your $150 hand-carved figures are increased in price by 10 percent to $165 each. This increase allows you to spend more time on each piece, enhancing the quality of the workmanship and, thus, increasing its value. Then, as increased value builds more sales, you can raise your prices again to reflect the enhanced value.

Understanding Regional Pricing

There's one more aspect of pricing your craft that you should consider before we get into pricing specific products: regional pricing. The price you get for decoupage crafts in suburban Chicago should be higher than the price you'll get in rural Alabama. Why? Many reasons.

First, folks in a large city will probably have more discretionary income, or money they can spend on the finer things in life than people living in rural areas. Second, the cost of materials may be higher in the big city. Third, the cost of labor is typically higher in the city; it costs more to live and work there. Fourth, rural areas are more likely to have native craftsmen who will compete with you.

How much of a factor is region in pricing? Craft prices are typically about 10 percent less in rural areas than in medium-sized cities, and about 5 to 10 percent more in metropolitan areas. In some areas of the South where economic conditions are lower, craft prices are about 20 percent less than medium-sized cities.

So there can be a 30 percent difference in prices for the same craft product between suburban Chicago and the rural South. Actually, there can be even more—or less—depending on other factors. But these approximations can help you in setting a studio rate and unit price for your craft depending on where you are selling your products.

Remember that this regional price difference is based on where the products are sold, not where they are made. That's why many crafters in the rural South and Midwest try to sell their products in larger cities in the North and West. Life isn't necessarily any better or worse in any of these regions. People are simply more prepared to pay higher prices in some locations than others. The smart crafter will consider these regional pricing differences in selling his or her products.

CHAPTER TWO

How to Price Popular Crafts

Popular crafts are those that you see most often as you visit craft shows across the nation. They are the crafts that many people think of when considering a gift for another or a hobby for themselves.

Most crafters try popular crafts first. These crafts typically require skills that can be learned in a short time, yet offer opportunity for unique expressions of artistry. Materials are easy to find. Designs and instructions are commonly available, as are experienced teachers. Most importantly, they're fun.

Popular crafts include floral crafts and wreaths, gift baskets, paper crafts, leatherwork, beading, candle and wax crafts, stained and etched glass, leaded glass, decoupage, tole painting, decorative painting, dough art, cake decorating, wedding crafts, woodcrafts, birdhouses, dollhouses, frames and mixed media crafts.

Popular crafts offer many crafters their first opportunity to learn about pricing their work. Whether you make popular crafts or those that require more tools and experience, learning how to price popular crafts will help you price your own work.

Basics of Pricing Popular Crafts

Pricing popular crafts is a craft unto itself. How can you price your popular craft? Begin by figuring your production cost. Calculate your materials costs. Establish a realistic studio rate. Calculate your overhead costs. Ensure yourself a reasonable profit. Market smart, selling value instead of price. We will cover all of these topics in this chapter.

One other thing: Learn from others. Study what other popular crafters are charging for their products. Develop friendships with non-competing popular crafters and share information with them. Join a local or national craft guild, especially one with members in your region or your craft. The American Craft Council (72 Spring St., New York, NY 10012; 212-274-0630) is a good place to start. From there you can join a state craft guild or art council.

Costing Materials

One good thing about pricing popular crafts is that the materials are readily available. You can find the majority of your materials at a local or regional craft supply store. Mail-order craft suppliers will also have nearly everything you need. And, as you've learned, competition breeds lower prices.

An excellent resource for craft supplies is Margaret Boyd's book, *The Crafts Supply Sourcebook* (Betterway Books). It includes more than 2,500 mail-order suppliers of crafts materials. Learn to buy wisely. The lower your materials cost, the more potential you have for profit from your crafts.

Estimating Overhead

As we said in chapter one, overhead is the cost of things that don't go into your product, but are necessary in making it. Overhead includes rent, tools, taxes, etc. Every crafter has overhead. If your craft is a hobby, you absorb the overhead yourself. If your craft will be sold to others, making it a small business, the cost of overhead can be passed on to your customers.

How can you keep overhead costs down? Keep tool costs to a minimum. Don't go out and rent a studio or retail store just yet. Budget the income from your crafts. Keep track of the money you earn from your craft as well as the money you spend.

Setting Studio Rates

The pricing of popular crafts varies tremendously because the material costs and time requirements vary between crafts and individual crafters. The studio rate (labor + overhead + profit) for a simple craft produced from a common design may be $25 to $30 an hour while a more complex and unique popular craft may near $40 to $45 an hour. Few makers of popular crafts have a studio rate of more than $45.

Your studio rate depends much on the originality of the design from which you produce your crafts. That is, if your craft is similar to the mass-produced products available at discount department stores, your studio rate will be much lower than if your crafts are distinctive. Why? Because prospective buyers compare price to value. A shopper seeing two items of similar design considers their value to be similar and expects the same of the price. So even if you have three times as much work in your craft as a similar mass-produced product, you will get a similar price for it. To earn the best studio rate for your craft, make it as original as you can. Be creative.

Ensuring Profit

How can you ensure profit from your popular crafts? Simply receive more than you spend. I know it sounds too simple, but it's the first rule of business. Since profit is the difference between what you receive and what you spend, increasing sales or decreasing expenses increases profits.

It's a balancing act. If you spend too little on materials or overhead expenses, your product may be less salable. If you try to increase profits by charging more than the customer will pay, you won't sell as much and profits drop. That's why I recommend that anyone starting to sell a product or service do so on a small scale. Here are some of my reasons:

1. We learn more from our mistakes than our successes
2. Mistakes cost money
3. Mistakes made in a small business cost less than those made by a big business

Go ahead and make some mistakes, as long as they are inexpensive and you can learn something valuable from each. Then, when your craft enterprise is larger, you'll make fewer and relatively less costly mistakes.

Selling Value

In the more competitive fields of crafts and folk art, selling value over price will help you compete with other crafters without having to resort to deep price cutting. As covered in chapter one, there are many ways you can sell value over price.

What is the value of your product? Make a list of the features and benefits that your craft product gives customers. For example, a picture frame's value will include:

- sturdy construction (feature) to last many generations (benefit)
- hand-carved edge (feature) for a decorative look (benefit)
- unique design (feature) that will be treasured for many years (benefit)

Remember, whenever price is discussed, take the opportunity to sell value. Don't assume that the customer sees all of the features and recognizes the benefits of purchasing your craft product over someone else's. Point them out.

Floral Crafts and Wreaths

Visit any craft show, weekend marketplace, or resort, and you'll find floral crafts and wreaths for sale. In many regions, they are the most popular of the popular crafts. If you make and sell floral crafts, the bad news is that you'll have many competitors driving the price down. The good news is that people are buying them and, if you can add value to your crafts, your competition will diminish and you can get a better price for what you love to do.

Studio Rate

Due to the number of competitors, the studio rate for floral crafts is typically lower than other crafts. The rate is also lower because it is relatively inexpensive for you, and your competitors, to start selling floral crafts. Most work is done by hand, requiring few tools and little financial investment beyond materials. Typical studio rates for floral crafts range from $20 to $30 an hour for experienced crafters with popular or creative designs. Less established crafters set their studio rate as low as $15 an hour until they find a niche and develop their skills.

For example, let's assume that a floral wreath requires $4 in materials and 30 minutes of time to craft. How should it be priced? Add your studio rate for one-half hour ($12.50, as an example) to the cost of materials ($4) for a cost price of $16.50. Add your profit and any sales costs for the final price. If your profit is 20 percent of cost, add $3.30 for a wholesale price of $19.80. If you're selling the wreath yourself, add 50 to 100 percent of wholesale to come up with the retail price of $29.70 to $39.60. Use odd pricing as described in chapter one to set these retail prices at $29.95 and $39.95.

But what if your competitors aren't charging anywhere near that much for a similar wreath? Drop your price? No! Sell value. Be creative and make your wreath so unique that the customer doesn't view it as having many competitors. Another option is to find a lower cost source of materials. Or, become more efficient, reducing the time required to make your wreath.

Gift Baskets

Over the last few years, gift baskets have become the craze. These baskets include a decorative collection of products selected and displayed around a specific theme: wines and cheeses for the romantic; baseball cards and games for youngsters; exotic foods for a hostess; craft items; or even gag gifts. The problem is, unless you're creative, your gift baskets will be competing with those in the deli or produce section of the supermarket.

Creative gift baskets include one or more core products that are unique to the designer. Many gift baskets include a teddy bear so yours should have a toy cat, armadillo or green gorilla with a bow in her hair.

Studio Rate

Your studio rate for gift baskets is typically lower than any other craft because customers believe that you simply throw a few things in a basket and tie a bow on it. Despite their oversight, gift baskets typically earn a studio rate of about $20 an hour. To earn a higher rate, be creative.

One successful crafter selects kitchen crafts from local shows for her gift baskets. Her finished baskets look great in the middle of a dining room table or on the end of a kitchen counter.

Paper Crafts

Paper crafts offer an excellent opportunity for individuals who want to make some money without a large investment in tools or materials. Popular paper crafts include paper making, custom greeting cards, origami, montages, paper maché and tissue craft. Materials typically cost less than 20 percent of your retail price, designs are often unique, and the tools required are minimal and inexpensive. Time and creativity are the most important components of your craft.

Studio Rate

The studio rate for popular paper crafts is $25 to $45 an hour, depending on creativity, artistry and competition. A few artisans earn as much as $55 an hour for their creative skills. Paper crafts that compete with store products typically earn a lower studio rate than those that the customer immediately identifies as being unique. Hand-made papers and custom cards face more competition with retail products, therfore earning lower studio rates. More distinctive paper crafts earn higher studio rates.

In any case, helping your customers understand the value and benefits of your paper crafts will grant you higher prices for your skills.

Leatherwork

Leather has been a popular material for thousands of years. Leather crafts, however, go through cycles of popularity. Though leatherwork is not as popular now as it has been in the past, interest is resurging. Crafters with leatherworking skills can earn a fair studio rate and the admiration of customers.

Studio Rate

Today's crafters who offer unique designs not found in retail stores can establish higher studio rates than those who compete with discount stores. Typical studio rates for leather crafters making wallets, purses and checkbook covers are in the $25 to $35 an hour range. More unique products like leather vests, gloves and other apparel earn $30 to $45 an hour. Those who custom tool western boots and belts typically establish a studio rate of $35 to $55 an hour. As with other crafts, those with less than a year's experience in the craft use a lower studio rate.

To earn higher studio rates, leather crafters develop unique designs, more efficient production methods, and build their name over many years.

Beading

Beading is a popular craft that offers many opportunities for creativity. Unfortunately, beading is labor-intensive. It takes a lot of time and patience to make jewelry and apparel from tiny beads. In addition, some customers unfairly compare custom bead work to imported products found in gift stores. So a bead crafter must work efficiently and creatively to earn a fair studio rate and price for products. Many make their own paper and fabric beads for more inventive products.

Studio Rate

Though new bead crafters are forced to set a studio rate of $20 an hour or less, experienced and efficient beaders can earn an hourly rate of up to $30. Few bead crafters earn more until they turn to exotic materials and fancy jewelry.

The key to making a fair price on bead crafts is to work efficiently. Study the work of others. Learn shortcuts that don't reduce quality or aesthetics. Practice. Develop your own singular designs that you can easily modify into new designs. The more efficient you become, the higher your studio rate can rise.

Candle and Wax Crafts

Put a string through wax and you have a candle. Simple enough. So why are many candle and wax crafters making higher studio rates than other popular crafts? They are creative.

For example, one successful wax crafter specializes in figurines of dogs and cats. Using molds, colored waxes and some hand tooling, she produces wax figures that look almost lifelike. They sell quickly to pet lovers. Before she found her niche, she made $36 an hour making candles. Her wax pets earn a studio rate of $50 an hour. In addition, she creates custom wax figures at $60 an hour. She now has a studio in a resort town, making and selling wax pets as well as a line of unique candles.

Studio Rate

A typical studio rate for candle and wax crafts is $25 to $35 an hour. Once the craftperson develops creative designs and a strong market, the sky's the limit.

Look at your own candle and wax products, then at those of your competitors. How can you make potential customers see the greater value in your products?

Stained and Etched Glass

Staining and etching glass have been popular crafts for hundreds of years. Glass becomes a canvas for creativity and self-expression, offering craftspeople a fair return for their time and talents.

Stained-glass products include windows (of course), sun catchers, wall hangings, lampshades, jewelry, jewelry boxes, frames and many other colorful items. Etched-glass products include glasses, bowls, plates, cups, jars and even windows.

Studio Rate

The studio rate for stained-glass work begins at $30 an hour and goes up to $65, depending on skill, originality and tools required. A common studio rate for stained glass work is $35. Etched-glass work follows a similar studio rate structure, or slightly less because the tools are typically less expensive. More important to the studio rate is the distinctive quality of the design. Stenciled etched glass, for example, earns a much lower studio rate than glass etched from unique or limited designs.

Once a studio rate is established, many glass crafters develop rules of thumb to make pricing easier. For example, a stained-glass product may be priced by the number of panes or panels or by the square inch. One crafter prices stained windows at $125 a square foot. Another prices a window at $6 per panel.

An etched-glass product can be priced by the square inch or square foot, depending on the product. The price for etched windows will typically range from $25 to $75 per square foot. Dining glassware may be priced per serving, ranging from $15 to $100 per unit depending on the design and the reputation and skill of the craftsperson.

Leaded Glass

Though similar to stained and etched glass crafts, leaded glass is typically a simpler craft requiring fewer tools and talents. That's not to say that leaded glass is easy to craft.

Pricing leaded-glass products depends on many factors. The most important being your skill and creativity. You not only want to make quality products, you want to make them distinct from the leaded mirrors and glass products sold at discount stores. Coming up with a new design takes some ingenuity, and making a high-quality product requires expertise.

Studio Rate

Studio rates for leaded-glass craftwork range from about $25 an hour for mass-produced products to about $55 an hour for glass pieces designed and produced for specific clients. Many lead-glass crafters produce competitively priced entry-level products, then offer custom design and craft work to discriminating clients.

Decoupage

Decoupage is a craft that surges in popularity once every generation. It is beginning its latest resurgence and offers creative craftspeople a reasonable income.

Decoupage, French for "cutting out," is the craft of decorating surfaces by gluing down paper cutouts, then varnishing over the design. Tools and materials are inexpensive. But quality decoupage is an art as well as a craft, earning the artisan/crafter a fair studio rate.

Studio Rate

Depending on skill, experience, efficiency and creativity, the studio rate for decoupage will typically range from $30 to $45 an hour. Those learning the craft set a studio rate of $20 to $30 an hour until they fully developed their skills.

Some decoupage artists enhance their studio rate by developing a primary design, then making slight variations of it to produce individual pieces in less time. For example, one successful decoupage craftsman specializes in adding paper roses to jewelry boxes. He creates three sizes of roses from a single rose design, cutting out components for dozens of boxes at once. This production method lowers his production time, and he now charges $40 an hour as compared to his previous studio rate of $32.

Decorative Painting

There are many objects you can decorate with paint—wooden window boxes, table runners, ceramic pitchers. They're often grouped into a single craft, decorative painting, because they share common skills and materials. A large segment of decorative painting is known as country folk painting. You can also use textural gel and acrylic paints to produce textured paintings.

Studio Rate

Decorative painters can often get a higher studio rate than other popular crafts, depending on their technique. Painting flowers on wooden blanks, obviously, requires less skill than painting realistic carved decoys. Basic painting skills typically earn a studio rate of $25 to $30 an hour while advanced skills earn $35 to $40 an hour. Creative and signature designs add $5 to $10 an hour to each of these studio rates.

An excellent resource for those wanting to start or advance in this craft is *Decorative Artist's Workbook* magazine (F&W Publications). It includes articles, tips, illustrations and supply sources for a wide variety of decorative painting projects.

Tole Painting

Tole painting is decorative painting on tin (tole means "sheet of iron" in French). It's an old craft still popular for making new things look old.

Studio Rate

If you have the talents to tole paint, you can typically earn a studio rate of $25 to $40 an hour. If you're just learning the craft, $15 to $25 an hour is a more realistic rate until you develop your skills and efficiency.

One successful craftsperson in the Pacific Northwest specializes in painting saw blades. Many people tole paint ciruclar saw blades, but Frank paints murals on antique lumberjack saws. His toled saws hang in restaurants, chambers of commerce, one even hangs in a museum. Frank's skills and reputation reflect his many years of tole painting experience. His studio rate is $50 an hour with a typical blade taking about an hour a foot to paint. Frank adds value to his salesmanship by dressing as a lumberjack when selling at craft shows and visiting galleries.

Dough Art

Dough art is a general term for forming objects using flour or cornstarch and binders to hold them together. Dough is a medium similar to clay. What can you make from dough? Kitchen magnets, miniatures, ornaments, fruits and vegetables, baskets and a variety of other handcrafted objects are popular dough crafts.

Studio Rate

The studio rate for dough art depends on product and its niche. Kitchen magnets that look like they came from a discount store will earn a lower studio rate than unique dough art products. The range is from about $20 an hour up to $40 an hour, with the scale increasing with creativity. One successful dough artist produces miniature computers from baker's clay, even painting the monitor's screen. Her studio rate is $35 an hour because her designs are unlike anything her customers have seen.

Cake Decorating

While we're in the kitchen, let's consider making a cake. Actually, cake decorating does not require baking skills. If you're not a baker, you can use packaged mixes or even buy the cake and icing from a baker, then decorate it yourself.

Cake decorating is an art requiring a creative eye and a steady hand—or two. Fortunately, you can develop your skills using basic tools and cardboard cake models to create and execute your designs. You can draw your designs on the cardboard pieces and then practice decorating. In fact, until you've developed a photo album of successfully decorated cakes, your cardboard cakes can be used to illustrate your ideas and talent to prospective customers.

Studio Rate

Cake decorators typically charge by the size of the cake as well as the complexity of the design. Both factors relate to time. You may price your cakes by the diameter of the cake's base and the number of tiers. Or you may multiply the cost of materials by a markup price, such as five or six. In any case, your price is established using your studio rate. The common studio rate for cake decorators is $20 to $30 an hour. As discussed in chapter one, you may establish a higher studio rate if your skills merit the increase and your clientele is willing to pay your price.

Wedding Crafts

Weddings require more crafts than cakes. Some crafters specialize in producing hand-crafted wedding mementos for guests, decorations for the reception, or even the bride and groom set for the top of the cake.

The more emotional the event, the less concern for price, a statement particularly true of weddings. People who will spend an entire weekend trying to save $100 on a car purchase will happily buy $500 in decorative crafts for just one weekend. This fact doesn't mean crafters can charge any price for wedding crafts. It means customers will pay a fair price for craftsmanship without quibbling.

Studio Rate

What studio rate should you set for your wedding crafts? Charge about the same as for related non-wedding crafts. That is, your studio rate for floral crafts or candle crafts will be the same whether or not the product is for a wedding. The difference being you can typically get a higher price for crafts produced for a wedding, allowing you to spend more time on design and production.

Woodcrafts

Pricing woodcrafts is an extensive topic that warrants its own book: *The Woodworker's Guide to Pricing Your Work* (Betterway Books) by Dan Ramsey, the author of this book. The book covers pricing craft and folk art, wood carving and turning, as well as furniture and cabinetry. It offers specific pricing guidelines, rules of thumb and shop rates for a variety of woodworking crafts.

Birdhouses

If you have limited woodworking tools and experience, wooden birdhouses are an excellent entry-level product. They can be constructed of inexpensive materials using basic tools, and they are very popular. Popularity means higher competition which minimizes profits. However, if you can develop an unusual design or a simplified method of constructing birdhouses, you can be certain this craft will be both profitable and fun.

Studio Rate

Pricing birdhouses is not difficult. Simple birdhouses of cedar can be sold for as little as $10 while ornate bird condominiums with hand-painting will sell for $200 or more. A studio rate of $30 to $40 per hour is typical for birdhouse builders. They often multiply material costs by three to calculate a retail price or by two for a wholesale price. That is, a birdhouse requiring $12 in materials is typically sold to a wholesaler for about $24 or directly to the customer for $36. The wholesaler will probably mark up the birdhouse twice and sell it for $48. So, in this example, you can set your retail price between $36 and $48 depending on how you are selling it, how much it costs you to sell it, and what your competitors are charging.

One way to earn a higher price is to develop a nontraditional birdhouse design or one that simulates an antique design. A nontraditional design would be a birdhouse that looks like the White House, your state's capitol or your city's municipal offices. Or you can copy a birdhouse design from a vintage catalog. The less your woodworking product looks like your competitors' products, the higher you can price it.

Some birdhouse builders also make and sell bird feeders and bird baths. Customers interested in birdhouses may also buy these products at the same time, increasing your income and reducing your selling costs. Or you can make and sell wooden birdcages of either modern or Victorian design. The studio rate and multiplier on these woodworking products are the same as for birdhouses.

Dollhouses

Some of the most popular categories of woodworking products are dollhouses and other children's toys. Dollhouses require a minimal investment in stock. In fact, some woodworkers build them out of the scrap from making larger projects, or they collect other woodworkers' scrap.

Studio Rate

There are many designs that can be constructed in a short time while offering the woodworker a fair studio rate. A studio rate of $25 to $45 an hour is typical, depending on the creativity of the design and the efficiency of the studio. Because making dollhouses requires more labor than other woodworking products, the markup is typically higher. Many dollhouses and other wooden toys are priced at four times the cost of materials. Of course, if you find your materials for free, estimate their retail cost for your price scale.

If you're making dollhouses, also consider making the furniture to go in them. Depending on skills, tools and the market, the studio rate for dollhouse furniture will range from $30 to $50 an hour. It's a broad range because the market is broad. Also, much depends on your investment in tools. Power tools for miniature woodworking are not as expensive as standard tools, but they are still expensive. You also need more of them. On the plus side, you can set up a woodworking shop for dollhouses and furniture in a spare room or shed rather than take over half of the garage.

Frames

Making and selling wooden picture frames is a lucrative business, especially if you can find a niche that allows you to develop a market of repeat customers. Some picture frame makers sell directly to the public, framing art or other items for display. Others manufacture frames for others to sell as components (such as in a frame shop) or as part of an artistic product (such as in an art gallery).

Frames are labor intensive. A frame maker might take the basic frame stock through six or more operations before arriving at the final product. Each operation may require a new setup. Finished frames will then sell from $25 to as much as $300 each depending on size, design, finish and value. As with other popular crafts, singular design raises the perceived value and the eventual price.

Studio Rate

Making frames requires advanced woodworking skills and tools for higher studio rates, but you can start with basic tools and skills while learning the trade. Picture frame makers establish studio rates of $35 to $40 an hour for jobs requiring only basic tools and skills, moving up to $45 or $50 an hour for custom frame production. Some frame craftspeople earn as much as $60 an hour for their studio rate.

Another way to create unique frames is to utilize uncommon woods. One successful frame maker uses myrtlewood, an evergreen with a fine grain, in making specialized frames. Others use regional hardwoods, selling their frames in markets where such woods are difficult to find.

Mixed Media Crafts

The best way to define "mixed media crafts" is "one from column A and two from column B." Mixed media crafts combine two or more crafts. For example, incorporate your decorative painting into a gift basket, add handmade candles to your floral wreaths or even make etched-glass decorations for the top of a wedding cake. Be creative!

Of course, pricing mixed media crafts can be a problem. The solution is to estimate the materials, time and studio rate for each craft element separately, then combine them for the final price. It's a little more work, but worthwhile. Remember, your creative merging of two crafts adds value as well as reduces competition. Your studio rates and your product price can be higher than for the individual craft products.

CHAPTER THREE

How to Price Needle and Fabric Crafts

Needle and fabric crafts have been popular for millenniums. Though technology has mechanized the production of daily wear, thousands of women and men still use their hands and skills to make garments and decorations with needle and fabric.

This chapter offers specific pricing guidelines for needle and fabric craftspeople who want to earn profit from their talents. We will cover hand weaving, loom weaving, needlepoint, quilts, lace, knitting, embroidery, cross-stitch, fiber crafts, dolls, teddy bears and puppets, silkscreen, spinning, macrame, rugs, basketry and other fabric crafts. None of these crafts will grant you great financial rewards, but offering your artistry to others can be rewarding. Reading this chapter can help you make a few bucks, too.

Basics of Pricing Needle and Fabric Crafts

Needle and fabric crafts are labor intensive. That is, the time required to produce these crafts is worth much more than the materials. Three dollars worth of fabric can be crafted into a product selling for ten times as much. So efficiency is important to pricing. The faster and more efficient you can silkscreen a blouse or stitch and assemble a doll, the more you will be paid per hour.

You can learn much about pricing your needle or fabric craft by visiting larger craft shows in your region. Take a small notebook, study what other craftspeople are doing and how they are pricing their work, and make notes on how you can improve on it. In studying a product, you might see a way to produce it better or faster. Don't copy; adapt.

Another way to learn others' pricing methods is to join an association like the American Quilter's Society (P.O. Box 3290, Paducah, KY 42002), Doll Makers Association (6408 Glendale St., Metairie, LA 70003), Handweavers Guild of America (120 Mountain Ave., Bloomfield, CT 06002) or Knitting Guild of America (P.O. Box 1606, Knoxville, TN 37901). Check a resource such as *The Encyclopedia of Associations* (Gale Research) for other organizations you may want to join.

Costing Materials

You can reduce the costs of the materials in your craft by shopping wisely. There are many suppliers of materials for needle and fabric crafts, and competition creates discounts. As you calculate the cost of materials, make sure you calculate all costs, including the price of gasoline or automotive mileage to pick up materials, or the shipping and handling costs of materials delivered.

If you buy your supplies by mail, read *The Crafts Supply Sourcebook* by Margaret Boyd (Betterway Books) for a list of suppliers to your craft.

As you establish the cost of materials for your craft product, develop and use rules of thumb. You may discover that the cost of materials for your product should be about 12 percent of the retail price or 25 percent of the wholesale price. Some labor-intensive crafts use a retail markup of 1000% to the cost of materials: a quilt with $30 in materials could be marked up this way for a retail price of $300.

Estimating Overhead

Your overhead costs for needle and fabric crafts relate to the amount and cost of tools you need to perform your craft. The tools for many of these crafts are relatively inexpensive and can be purchased for less than $100. However, looms, industrial sewing machines and other machines can cost $1,000 or more.

By tracking the cost of tools and how long you expect them to last, you can determine their value. You may establish that your tools are minimal and cost you only $3 an hour for purchase, maintenance and replacement. That's $3 for each hour of use. Or if you have an expensive loom, you might estimate that it adds another $7 an hour to your overhead. In any case, you must know the cost of your tools in order to set your fees and ensure savings for tool repair or replacement when the time comes.

Setting Studio Rates

How much should your studio rate (labor + overhead + profit) be? Much depends on your skills, efficiency, creativity and required tool cost. Let's look at an example.

Joan Simoni makes hand puppets. When she started selling her puppets two years ago, Joan established a studio rate of $25 an hour because she mass-produced three puppet designs using an old industrial sewing machine she picked up cheap. Today, she gets $30 an hour for the same work—and she is more proficient so her wholesale prices are about the same. But Joan has added a new line of signature puppets. For this line, Joan established a studio rate of $40 an hour.

A new competitor began selling to Joan's customers at a lower price. How did Joan respond? She could have dropped the mass-produced line and concentrated on the puppets with the higher studio rate. Instead, Joan found a way to reduce her studio rate on the mass-produced puppet line without reducing profits. Joan hired her college-age daughter who needed some extra income while at school. Joan established a studio rate of $20 an hour for her daughter's work, reducing costs and allowing her to profitably compete. It also helped her daughter earn some money. Joan then concentrated her efforts on the creative line of puppets.

Your studio rate will depend on skills, competition, originality, tool requirements and your ability to sell value.

Ensuring Profit

Because needlework and fiber crafts are labor intensive, multipliers and markups are somewhat different from other craft products. The stock may only cost 10 percent of the wholesale price of the finished item—$4 for materials that will become a product priced at $40 wholesale or $80 retail. Tools and related overhead may add another 5 percent of wholesale. The labor may be about 75 percent of the wholesale price. The $80 retail item may require an hour to produce at a studio rate of $30 an hour. The cost is now $36 ($4 materials + $1.50 overhead + $30 labor = $35.50). A $40 wholesale price will allow for a profit of 10 percent of wholesale or $4. In this example, percentages would be:

	OF WHOLESALE	OF RETAIL
Materials	10%	5.0%
Overhead	5%	2.5%
Labor	75%	37.5%
Profit	10%	5.0%
Sales Costs		50.0%
Totals	100%	100%

Selling Value

Value is the worth of something, often measured in dollars. A buyer decides a product's value depending on its usefulness and importance. Value is also established by comparing the product's benefits to those of similar products.

So you can see what you need to do to sell the value of your needle or fabric crafts: Help the buyer understand the product's usefulness and importance. That is, sell him or her on the benefits. For example:

> *"This is a one-of-a-kind lace centerpiece that depicts the budding of roses in spring. There are no other lace pieces like it in the world."*

> *"Your friends will admire the intricate detail of this quilt that follows the old-world style."*

> *"This vibrantly colored silkscreen depicts the Umpqua lighthouse just a few miles from here. It will be a lifetime souvenir of your stay on the Oregon coast."*

Help the buyer see the value of your work and you will sell more.

Hand Weaving

Hand weaving seems to be a lost art. One reason is that handweavers don't get enough money for their efforts. They frequently earn below minimum wage for their craft because they have difficulty getting a good price when competing with mass-produced products.

What's the answer? Two answers: Work efficiently and sell value. Crafters converting hobbies to small businesses must rethink how they produce items. Weaving time cannot be based on how long it takes while watching TV. It must be based on concentrating on the job at hand and working as efficiently as possible. In addition, hand-woven products must emphasize the quality craftmanship so buyers can see the difference between your product and that available at retail stores. How you emphasize the difference depends on what you're weaving. Some weavers select higher quality fibers while others produce detailed designs.

Studio Rate

What is a realistic studio rate for hand weavers? Those with experience who work efficiently and craft unique products can establish a studio rate of $20 to $35 an hour. Those with less experience may set a rate at $15 an hour and work up to $40 an hour once they build a reputation for quality. Remember to work efficiently and sell value.

Loom Weaving

Production loom weaving is priced differently, as you must calculate the cost of the loom into your overhead. However, a production loom also offers many weavers a higher hourly studio rate because of the loom's efficiency. For example, a loom weaver who can sustain a pace of 60 picks a minute for hours at a time can earn a studio rate of $30 an hour or more, depending on consumer appeal for the product.

To make more money, be creative.

Needlepoint

The difficulty in profitably selling your needlepoint work is you're competing with crafters who sell their work for the cost of materials. Their studio rate is zero. How can you compete with them?

First, develop your own creative needlepoint style and designs. What local landmarks can you depict in your designs to help make your products unique? Your goal is to establish and promote a style that is uniquely yours, thereby reducing competition. Winning awards helps.

Studio Rate

Depending on your skills and those of competitors, your studio rate may be $15 to $40 an hour. In order to successfully sell, many needlepointers set an initial hourly studio rate of about $20 until the market recognizes their creativity. They can then slowly increase the studio rate.

Finally, sell value. Help your customers see the difference between your work and that of others. You won't tear down your competitors, you'll build the value of your work in the customer's mind.

Quilts

Quilts are a traditional favorite at craft shows and fairs. A quilt rack can prominently display numerous quilts, inviting close inspection. They often sell themselves.

Colorful and creative designs are the key to selling quilts. Some quilters specialize in original Sioux designs, vintage fabrics, calicos, textured fabrics or modern designs. Others quilt pillows, stuffed toys or murals.

Studio Rate

Though quilting is labor intensive, an experienced quilter can use tools and templates to increase efficiency and thereby increase the studio rate. A typical studio rate for quilters is slightly higher than for other fabric and needle crafts. An experienced quilter can set a studio rate of $30 an hour and earn as high as $50 an hour after developing a following. Less experienced quilters start off at about $20 an hour.

These studio rates may sound high if you're used to quilting for minimum wage or less. Keep in mind that a studio rate includes both labor and overhead. Once you begin selling your products, you must work more efficiently. You can't earn $30 an hour quilting while watching TV. Invest in tools that make your job easier. You must be focused. If you dislike producing quilts or other crafts at this pace, factor your desired efficiency into your studio rate. You may establish a "soap-opera rate" at 50 percent of your standard studio rate.

Lace

Making lace has become so mechanized that those who make it by hand cannot financially compete with machine-made or even some imported hand lace. However, if you use lace in an imaginative way, you can still make a profit with it. One lace maker designs and produces lace figures to sit atop computer monitors. These figures are shaped as angels in white lace and devils in red lace. They became so popular at craft shows that she developed related desktop lace products: coffee cup doilies, lace monitor trim and lace-covered pen holders.

Studio Rate

Creative lace can earn a studio rate of $25 to $30 an hour. Many lace crafters increase their income by improving efficiency and developing shortcuts that don't reduce quality.

Knitting

Knitting is a popular needle craft in which many people want to turn their skills into income. As with other crafts, the key to making money with knitting is to offer a product of distinct value. When first made and sold, knitted toilet tissue covers were unique. Today, their popularity and price have fallen. As a crafter, you need to imagine tomorrow's popular knitted craft product. What yarns will be popular? Find a product that you enjoy knitting and that others will enjoy using.

As with knitting, crocheting is not as profitable as other crafts. However, signature designs and fine quality will always attract customers and increase prices. The price you earn depends on your skills, tools, designs and competition.

Studio Rate

Depending on your product, knitting typically earns a studio rate of $20 to $30 an hour for experienced craftspeople. Knitters can become more efficient, thereby increasing their studio rate, by using a knitting machine for some or all of their work. Some knitters have two or more studio rates, depending on the skills and tools required. The lower rate is for popular mass-produced products and the higher rate is for those items that require greater creativity.

Embroidery

Embroidery offers many opportunities for creativity. Because of this, an experienced embroiderer can establish a studio rate of $25 to as much as $40 an hour, depending on skills and efficiency. Some crafters, for example, specialize in punch embroidery with metallic yarns. Others use Brazilian embroidery designs in their products.

Once established, an embroiderer can automate some steps to make production easier and faster. Automatic punch embroidery tools, for example, can produce up to five hundred stitches a minute. Other crafters customize their products using monogram equipment.

What designs and techniques can you come up with to make your embroidery more valuable to others?

Cross-Stitch

Most needle crafters have tried cross-stitch. Some love it and want to make a few dollars with their skill. But because cross-stitch is so popular, the competition is extensive and the studio rate is lower than other needle crafts.

Studio Rate

The typical cross-stitcher will have difficulty selling products with a studio rate above $25 an hour. There are just too many products sold by discount stores that look like handcrafted cross-stitch.

To increase your studio rate and your profits from cross-stitch crafts, be creative and sell value. One successful crafter specialized in transferring family photos into cross-stitched works of art. She found a method of imprinting cross-stitch fabrics with a photograph. She used the original photo as a visual aid in selecting yarn colors and cross-stitching the fabric. Because of her inventive idea, she was able to establish a higher studio rate than other cross-stitchers at $32 an hour.

Fiber Crafts

The process of refining fibers is a craft in itself. Most crafters who gather, spin and spool fibers sell their products as yarns and fabrics to other crafters. A few continue the process, making their own crafts from fibers they've produced.

How can you price fiber crafts? As covered in chapter one, the pricing process depends on both actual costs and perceived values. Textured fibers seem to get a higher price than those that look like fabric store products. Strive for creativity.

Studio Rate

Studio rates for fiber crafts range from $20 an hour for hand weaving to $35 or $40 an hour for producing exotic fabrics with the use of mechanized weaving looms.

Some fiber crafters also dye their craft to make the resulting fibers and products even more unique and valuable.

Dolls

Craft buyers know dolls can be priced at $5 or $500. That's good for you because it means fewer consumers will question a price that reflects a fair studio rate. If you decide to price your dolls at $125 each, you have a good chance of receiving it as long as you can demonstrate value.

Why can you ask this price? Because you're not competing with the discount stores that sell dolls for children. Most craft dolls are sold to adult collectors rather than for children's amusement. Your buyers can better afford your craftsmanship.

Of course, there are many types of dolls: porcelain, ceramic, jade, fabric, wooden and ever-popular plastic. You may make your own doll bodies and buy the clothing, or the other way around. Or you can do all of it. Remember: The more unique the design, the higher the price.

Studio Rate

Typical studio rates for doll crafters range from $25 an hour for mass-produced products to $55 or even $60 an hour for unique designs requiring special craft tools and equipment.

Teddy Bears and Puppets

Everyone loves teddy bears and puppets. For this reason, a creative crafter can appeal to customers' emotions for a better price and a higher studio rate than other fabric crafts. As with other crafts, if your stuffed animals look like those sold at discount stores for $7.95, that's about all you'll get for them. Spend a little more time on the design and production to net higher profits. In addition, "cute" sells faster.

For example, one puppet maker produced three different body designs, then added one of six head designs, bringing the available combinations up to eighteen. The crafter supplemented this wide selection by adding different colors of hair or ribbons to the heads, increasing the individual personality of each puppet. This allowed her to show about 30 puppets at craft shows without duplication. Of course, duplicates were stored under the counter to replace those that sold.

Sandy and Dan Kearney make their teddy bears out of old fur coats, recycling them for a new generation. Their prices range from $150 to $300 each, depending on the cost of the fur and the labor involved.

Studio Rate

Teddy bears and puppets earn crafters a typical studio rate of $30 to $40 an hour. Experienced crafters can increase their studio rate as they identify faster-selling products and demand goes up.

Silkscreening

Silkscreening and related crafts require few tools and are so popular that competition is high. Silkscreen t-shirts, for example, are mass-produced and can be purchased at most shopping malls. Crafters don't have a chance—unless they add value to their product. Unique designs, quality cloths and other elements can lift products above the competition.

Studio Rate

What's a fair studio rate for silkscreen work? With minimal tools and less than a year's experience, $15 to $20 an hour is typical. Add $5 to $10 an hour for creative designs or for products that require specialized equipment. A silkscreen artist can earn as much as $45 to $50 an hour for his or her efforts.

Tie-dying will earn about the same studio rate as silkscreening, with higher rates for creativity.

Spinning

Spinning yarn from wool, cotton, silk and other natural fibers is an ancient craft. The resulting yarns and threads are popular with other craftspeople who turn them into other products. So, in most cases, your customer is another crafter.

There are many aspects of spinning: selection of fiber, preparation, spinning and finishing. Depending on the fiber you spin, this process can be relatively easy or moderately difficult. You will be paid in direct proportion to the difficulty of the project and the level of skill required. Though the cost of spinning equipment is a factor in overhead costs, it relates to your efficiency. The more efficiently you spin, the more product you can sell.

Studio Rate

Spinners typically establish an initial studio rate of $20 to $30 an hour, depending on skills and efficiency. As your talents grow, you can increase your studio rate. A more accurate gauge of whether the studio rate should be changed is how well your product is selling. As covered in chapter one, if you are busier than you want to be, increase prices via your studio rate. If you're not quite busy enough, establish a studio rate on the lower end of the spectrum until business improves.

Macrame

Remember when every crafter did macrame? Macrame is a simple entry-level craft that ties knots in yarn to make decorative and useful products. Because of its simplicity and popularity, many crafters make and sell macrame. That means competition, and lots of it.

Fortunately, if macrame is your chosen craft, you can increase sales and your studio rate by adding value. How? Use exotic yarns, add unique designs or include a second craft such as beading to differentiate your products from those of your competitors.

Studio Rate

What's a fair studio rate for macrame crafters? Whatever you can get. In some regions, macrame plant hangers and wall decorations saturate the market so you should concentrate on tote bags or purses. Other regions have few crafters making plant hangers from colorful yarns, so there may be your niche. The more unique your products, the more money people will usually pay for them.

A common studio rate for experienced macrame crafters is $20 to $25 an hour. Those learning the craft may charge less for their first selling season while those who have developed a popular product line will get more.

Rugs

There are many ways to craft a rug. Some are punched, others are braided, many are hooked and a few are woven. Because there are many rug production methods, pricing rugs can be more difficult than other crafts.

Most successful rug crafters start by making and marketing smaller rugs until they learn what fits their skills and what sells. If you have numerous craft shows in your area, become an exhibitor and offer a variety of rugs.

Most important, talk with attendees and other exhibitors to learn what sells and why.

Studio Rate

As a guide, establish your studio rate based on your skills, your efficiency and demand in your market. Those punching smaller solid-color rugs or braiding rugs typically establish studio rates of $20 to $35 an hour. Rugs with designs in them require more time and skills, earning a slightly higher studio rate. The more intricate the design, the higher the rate.

Basketry

Basketry is a diverse craft with a wide variety of possible raw materials and even more diverse products. You can make flower baskets, picnic baskets, sewing baskets, clothes hampers, plant holders, trivets or a dozen other useful and decorative products. You can make them of cane, reed, wood, rush, husks or other materials.

Studio Rate

So how should you price your baskets? First, make sure that your baskets don't look like those available at discount stores. Second, remember that no one in recorded history has become rich by making and selling baskets, your studio rate will be on the lower end of the spectrum—$20 to $25 an hour—because, frankly, you're competing with fourth-generation basket makers in third-world countries. Unless your baskets are distinctive, your prices must be close to those of your competitors, foreign or domestic.

One successful basket crafter knew she couldn't beat her competition, so she joined them. Because so many of her customers at regional craft shows balked at her prices, she began selling a line of imported baskets to satisfy this type of customer. In addition to making sales she wasn't able to make before, she was also able to use the lower-priced baskets to illustrate the quality of her own basketry. She drew buyers in with price, then showed them quality and value.

Other Fabric and Needle Crafts

The list of fabric and needle crafts is extensive. How should you price your crafts if other than those in this chapter? As you've learned, fabric and needle crafts can earn a studio rate of anywhere from $20 to $50 or more per hour. Studio rates are based on creativity, uniqueness, required skills, competition and your ability to sell value.

Your time and your skills are valuable to others. Don't sell yourself short.

CHAPTER FOUR

How to Price Ceramic Crafts

Craft shows are incomplete without ceramic crafts. Ceramics are unique expressions of talent and skill that grace craft buyers with both beauty and function.

Ceramic crafts garner prices anywhere from two dollars for a clay blank up to thousands of dollars for a one-of-a-kind ceramic sculpture. Pricing ceramic crafts doesn't have to be a chore. It can be fun. It can offer you a fair return for your investment of time and skills. This chapter will show you how.

Basics of Pricing Ceramic Crafts

Ceramics are craft products made from clay and similar materials. Once molded into shape, potter's clay must be heated in a kiln to dry it and make it hard. Some synthetic clay compounds don't require a kiln for drying. In general, ceramics are crafts that are poured into molds, while pottery is shaped on a spinning pottery wheel. They are fired or dried in the kiln, then painted or glazed to seal and decorate the surface.

To the advantage of the crafter, ceramics offer a permanence that make fair pricing easier. Most craft buyers can see durability and artistic value in ceramic products. This is especially true for ceramics that aren't compared to those at discount stores.

What ceramic crafts are popular? Coffee cups, plates, flowerpots, vases, ashtrays, ornaments and refrigerator magnets are the most popular. Covered in this chapter are clay crafts, functional and decorative pottery and ceramics, cast plaster, earthenware, stoneware, porcelain and other ceramic crafts. In the coming pages you'll learn how to price each of these ceramic crafts as well as how to sell their value to your customers.

Costing Materials

Materials for ceramic crafters include: firing, nonfiring, modeling and other clays; finishes; glazes; decals and related materials that go into your craft products.

An excellent resource for craft supplies is Margaret Boyd's book, *The Crafts Supply Sourcebook* (Betterway Books). It includes more than 2,500 mail-order suppliers of craft materials, including eighty-five specifically for ceramic crafters.

To develop an accurate cost of the materials used in producing your ceramic products, use the Materials Purchase Record and Materials Use Record (see Appendix). It can help you determine the cost per item for your line of products, making pricing easier and ensuring profits. Without these facts you're just guessing.

Estimating Overhead

Overhead expenses—indirect costs of the product—are typically higher for ceramics and pottery than for other crafts. This is because the tools are more expensive. Kilns, especially, can be expensive. Pottery wheels aren't cheap either. Add to this the cost of related furnishing and equipment and you can see why ceramic crafters need more money to start and operate than others. This cost must be passed on, albeit slowly, to the consumer to ensure that the investment can continue.

Ceramics and pottery also require greater space than other crafts. That means you'll have to set aside part of the garage, an outbuilding or even space within your home to make your products. This area will require lighting, heat and power for your kiln, wheel or other equipment. If you make a profit from your part-time business, you'll be able to deduct the expenses for this area from your profits before paying taxes.

To minimize overhead in the beginning, consider using materials that don't require firing or glazing. Another option is to find someone who will let you rent their kiln for your work, charging by the firing. In fact, some craft studios rent kiln time.

Setting Studio Rates

Setting a fair studio rate (labor + overhead + profit) for your ceramic crafts is critical to making a reasonable amount of money for your time and skills. How can you set a fair studio rate? First, use guidelines passed on by other ceramicists. Part-time ceramic and pottery shops typically establish a studio rate ranging from $30 to $60 an hour. The lower end is for mass production of a few basic designs while the higher end is for experienced artisans producing custom products for a defined group of selective buyers. Those starting and learning the trade may establish an initial studio rate $5 to $10 per hour lower, but with a six to twelve month limit. After that, their studio rate should be at $30 an hour or more.

Ensuring Profit

Ceramics and pottery are labor-intensive crafts. Pricing and profits are different from other craft products. Ceramicists and potters typically spend more on materials and tools/overhead than fabric crafters, for example. The price of a typical ceramics or pottery product will break down like this:

	OF WHOLESALE	OF RETAIL
Materials	20%	10%
Overhead	10%	5%
Labor	60%	30%
Profit	10%	5%
Sales Costs		50%
Totals	100%	100%

For example, a coffee mug for which the materials cost $2 will typically become a finished product that will wholesale for $10 or retail for $20. In this example, about $6 will be charged to labor, which is 60% of wholesale ($10) or 30% of retail ($20). The $8 studio rate includes overhead, labor, and profit, which equals 80% of wholesale in the example. If your studio rate is $32 an hour, you should spend about 15 minutes producing this product. If you're spending more, review your price or your production methods. This time estimate is for efficient production, not leisurely hobby time.

Selling Value

Value is the worth of a product or service. Price is the amount of money given by the buyer in exchange for value. To increase the price, increase the value or make sure that the buyer recognizes the value of the product. Why wouldn't the typical buyer pay $300 for a ceramic figurine? Because the buyer doesn't believe the value to be $300.

How can you sell the value of your ceramics? One way, as discussed in chapter one, is to answer price questions with points of value.

"Yes, that figurine is priced at $300 because it is one of a kind and combines many hours of work with many years of skill. You'll remember the quality long after you've forgotten the price."

"Of course, discount stores have coffee cups for six bucks each. These coffee cups will outlast their's by many years, yet won't look like everyone else's."

"$200 does seem like a lot of money for a decorative plate. The plate itself is the finest bone china. The design is unique. I learned my craft during a ten-year apprenticeship to the finest ceramicist in Belgium who taught me to carefully blend the rose petals using a special finish. The piece is then carefully fired using imported glazes. The edging is hand-painted twenty-four-carat gold. This is a piece your grandchildren will treasure and enjoy."

Others sell on price. You sell on value!

Clay Crafts

People shopping for crafts usually don't know what they want until they see it. The advantage of clay crafts is they can be molded and finished to be anything from a functional plate to a whimsical figure.

Clay crafts are typically those that don't require firing in a kiln to harden. They are usually air dried. Many are formed by hand while others require a mold.

Studio Rate

Without a fired finish, many clay crafts don't look as valuable as those with a colorful hardened finish. This perception keeps the typical studio rate for clay crafts lower than for pottery and ceramics. The studio rate for clay crafts will usually begin at $20 to $25 an hour and top out at $35 an hour. The keys to the higher rate are value and quality.

Functional Pottery

Functional pottery is clay products molded by hand on a pottery wheel. Functional pottery products include flowerpots, plates, mugs, soup tureens, candlesticks, coasters, ashtrays and a variety of other useful items.

Because they are functional, most buyers will unconsciously compare your products to those available in retail stores. Your job is to help them see that the value of your products is greater than off-the-shelf functional pottery. As described in chapter one, you can make your products more distinctive. You can also point out the value difference to the customer. After all, you're not a store clerk, you're the crafter.

Studio Rate

A typical studio rate for functional pottery products is $25 to $35 an hour—slightly less for new crafters and slightly more for those who have built a following. Of course, the more efficiently you work, the more you can earn.

Decorative Pottery

Decorative pottery crafts are more easily distinguished from products at retail stores. Each craft item is made unique by a brushstroke or modified pigment. The purchase of a decorative pottery item is more impulsive than functional pottery, so the more your product appeals to the aesthetics of the buyer, the more buyers you will get.

Decorative pottery products include vases, figurines, planters and dozens of other creative items. You can express your imagination more freely with decorative pottery. To visualize this, simply visit a large craft show and view the wide variety of decorative pottery products on sale, then design some of your own.

Studio Rate

Because decorative pottery is perceived as more creative than functional pottery (though it may not be), the typical studio rate for the decorative potter is slightly higher. Depending on your region and competition, a typical studio rate for decorative potters is $30 to $50 an hour. Unique products and designs earn the higher rate, of course. Susan Wigglesworth makes Old World Santas from pottery, selling them at $40 each.

Functional Ceramics

Ceramics use clay poured into a mold to form the product. Many pottery products that can be formed by hand can also be formed by mold. In addition, cookie jars, mugs, ashtrays and clocks are popular ceramic crafts. Ceramic lamp bases can also be profitably made and sold.

Studio Rate

The studio rate for functional ceramics is slightly higher than for functional pottery. The typical rate is $30 to $40 an hour. The higher rate is established because most crafters can produce more products during an hour using a mold than by hand. Of course, much depends on the product and the market.

One method of setting your studio rate is to study your competitors at a craft show, analyzing their products and estimating their production time. From this "market research" you can probably estimate their studio rates. You may be quite surprised by the spectrum of rates you discover: anywhere from $10 to $50 an hour. Ignore the highest and lowest rates and concentrate on the range of your more successful competitors.

Decorative Ceramics

Decorative ceramics are popular crafts found at most craft shows. They include many of the same products made on a potter's wheel decorated with hand-painted embellishments, as well as Christmas ornaments, ornate pitchers and similar items.

The cookie jar is a popular ceramic product which is both decorative and functional. One craftsperson has developed a line of Three Bears cookie jars that has earned her an excellent income for a weekend business.

Studio Rate

Because of their popularity with buyers and efficiency for crafters, decorative ceramics earn a higher studio rate than functional ceramics. Many established crafters use a studio rate of $35 to $45 an hour to price their work, depending on creativity and efficiency.

Again, add value to your products to earn the best studio rate. Let your customers know why your products are a better value to them than those in retail stores. Use the Features and Benefits Worksheet at the end of this book to help sell value.

Cast Plaster

Many crafters who become potters or ceramicists start with plaster. Using molds they've made or purchased, crafters mix and pour a plaster compound that can then be air-dried and hand-painted or spray-painted. Common cast plaster products include figurines, clocks, plaques, magnets and picture frames. The most popular is figurines, with many crafters specializing in one or two types: angels; sports; animals; cowboys or caricatures.

Studio Rate

Because cast plaster crafts are easy to make, requiring minimal skills and equipment, the selling price is lower than for other ceramic crafts. Fortunately, efficiency can make up the difference, offering a fair studio rate of $25 to $35 an hour.

Some casters use resins or even cement to make their crafts. A successful casting shop in the Pacific Northwest specializes in casting and painting concrete deer. They even place plastic antler sets on the bucks to make them seem authentic and use a special paint that preserves a realistic color for many years. Their studio rate is $38 an hour for this specialized product.

Earthenware

Earthenware is a functional pottery made of fired, baked or dried clay formed by hand on a potter's wheel to look handcrafted. Earthenware dishes, cups, serving bowls and even cooking pots and utensils typically retain the natural colors of the clay. However, some are glazed.

Creative earthenware includes dishes with uneven edges and dishes made with clays unique to the region. The less your earthenware looks like other crafters', the more value it will have in the eyes of the customer.

Studio Rate

Because crafting earthenware requires lots of time and talent, the typical studio rate for the crafter can be higher than for other crafts. The starting studio rate is still about $25 an hour, but the rate for a popular earthen potter is $40 to $50 an hour, especially if the products are sold through galleries or are individually signed and numbered.

Stoneware

Stoneware is produced by a glazing and firing process that makes the finish look like glass. Stoneware typically uses denser clays than other wares. Quality dinnerware is often also known as stoneware. The process requires advanced skills, quality materials and more equipment than most ceramic crafts. As you would imagine, these factors translate to a higher studio rate than for other crafts.

Studio Rate

Stoneware crafters typically establish a studio rate of $35 to $50 an hour. However, because the quality of stoneware is difficult to identify when purchased, some stoneware crafters find themselves competing with retail stores. As with other crafters, those who can add and sell value will earn the higher studio rates.

Porcelain

Porcelain is similar to stoneware, except porcelain requires two primary firings. The biscuit firing, at a lower temperature, seals the ceramic material. The gloss firing, at a much higher temperature, gives the surface a glasslike finish. The porcelain process can be applied to dinnerware, figurines, clocks, ashtrays or nearly any other product made of clays. The glazes are more expensive and the process requires more refined skills.

Studio Rate

Porcelain crafters establish a studio rate of at least $35 to $50 an hour, with many established shops making more. Quality and efficiency are the main ingredients for higher studio rates.

Other Ceramic Crafts

The craft of ceramics is quite old, but the methods are simple. It is the process of forming soft clay or other materials into useful or decorative products, then allowing it to dry until hard. Some ceramic crafts are then finished with paint or baked-on glaze. Some products are more functional than others. Some are strictly decorative, but all must be appealing to the buyer.

Figure pricing by estimating material costs and establishing a fair studio rate. Be certain to help the buyer understand the quality of your work.

CHAPTER FIVE

How to Price Jewelry and Metal Crafts

Few can overlook the beauty of jewelry. These decorative adornments have been popular craft items since the Stone Age, and they're just as popular today.

This chapter will help you profitably price your jewelry and metal crafts including silver, gold, exotic metals, gems, hand jewelry, neck jewelry, clothing jewelry, forged metals, tinsmithing, coppersmithing, knives and cutlery and other metal crafts.

Basics of Pricing Jewelry and Metal Crafts

Too many crafters give their products away with a labor rate of only a few dollars an hour. Of course, the customer will not pay more than you ask for your crafts. The customer depends on you to determine the value of your work. If you only ask $10 for a fine piece, that's all you'll get. As discussed in chapter one, if you ask for $50 and explain the product's value to the customer, you will get $50. You must learn to set a reasonable price that gives you a fair wage yet stays within the range of what a customer can be persuaded to pay. In this chapter, you'll learn how to price jewelry and metal crafts: how to cost materials; set labor fees; estimate overhead; ensure a profit and sell value. You'll also learn what other crafters charge for their labor and products.

One excellent way of learning what others charge for their crafts is to join an association like the American Society of Gemcutters (P.O. Box 9852, Washington, DC 20016). Association membership includes access to the Gemcutters National Library and a subscription to *American Gemcutter*, as well as opportunities to attend regional and national meets to learn more about your craft. Metal crafters also have trade associations identified in craft magazines.

Costing Materials

Jewelry makers and metal crafters typically buy more expensive materials than other crafters. Therefore, it's important for you to develop economical and reliable sources of gems and metals. Once you have found good resources, keep looking because you'll want secondary sources in case the primary ones fail to serve your needs.

If you buy your jewelry and metalworking supplies by mail, read *The Crafts Supply Sourcebook* by Margaret Boyd (Betterway Books) for a list of suppliers to your craft.

Estimating Overhead

Your overhead costs for jewelry and metal crafts relate to the amount and cost of tools you need to perform your craft. Make a list of the tools you use and expect to use in producing your craft. By tracking the cost of tools and how long you expect them to last, you can determine their value. You may establish that your tools are minimal and cost you only $3 an hour for purchase, maintenance and replacement. That's $3 for each hour of use. Or needing special tools, you might estimate they add another $4 an hour to your overhead. In any case, you must know how much your tools cost in order to set your fees and ensure you have money for tool repair or replacement as necessary.

Setting Studio Rates

Studio rates (labor + overhead + profit) for jewelry crafters are typically from $35 to $60 an hour depending on many factors: skill; talent; tools and originality. A jeweler who uses basic tools to make identical angel pins may only earn $30 or $35 an hour. A goldsmith producing unique and exotic designs for galleries may set an hourly rate of $50 or more. Most jewelry and metalworkers will set an hourly rate somewhere in between, depending on skills, experience and the distinct quality of their design.

Also, much depends on the tools you use. A maker of clothing jewelry typically needs only a few basic tools. An investment of $100 may be all that's required. On the other hand, a maker of fine cutlery may require tools for forging and sharpening quality steel into blades; the investment in tools for this craft may be $1,000 or more. This is part of your craft venture's overhead and a component of your studio rate or labor fees.

Ensuring Profit

Because making jewelry and other metal crafts is such a labor-intensive craft, multipliers and markups are somewhat different from other craft products. The stock may only cost 20 percent of the wholesale price of the finished item—$10 for a gem and setting that will become a product priced at $50 wholesale or $100 retail. Tools and related overhead may add another 10 percent of wholesale. The labor may be about 60 percent of the wholesale price. The $100 retail item may require an hour to produce at a studio rate of $30 an hour. The cost is now $45 ($10 materials + $5 overhead + $30 labor = $45). A $50 wholesale price will allow for a profit of 10 percent of wholesale or $5. In this example, percentages would be:

	OF WHOLESALE	OF RETAIL
Materials	20%	10%
Overhead	10%	5%
Labor	60%	30%
Profit	10%	5%
Sales Costs		50%
Totals	100%	100%

Selling Value

Value is the worth of something, often measured in dollars. The buyer decides a product's value depending on its usefulness and importance. Value is also established by comparing the product's benefits to those of similar products.

So you can see what you need to do to sell the value of your jewelry or metal crafts. Help the buyer understand the product's usefulness and importance. Sell him or her on the benefits.

"This fine cutlery set will be passed on to your children and grandchildren who will appreciate your taste in quality."

"Maybe this is the ring that you will give to your grandchild when she becomes old enough to appreciate its value."

"Gold is a precious metal that speaks to everyone. Imagine how much pleasure you'll receive over the years from this pendant."

"A year from now, you'll have forgotten the price, but you'll be reminded daily of the value."

Many successful crafters help buyers visualize the work that's involved in producing their product by actually working while at craft shows. A cutlery crafter may have a foot-operated sharpening wheel that he uses to keep blades sharp—and to display his skills. A jeweler can draw people to her booth by showing how she makes her products.

Help the buyer see the value of your work and you will sell more.

Silver Crafts

People love silver jewelry and crafts so there's a lot of competition for their dollars.

Does this mean you shouldn't try to make and sell silver crafts? No. It means that you should design and craft original products from silver. If your products look like silver-plated imported items selling for five bucks, that's the price customers will expect to pay for them.

Studio Rate

The studio rate for silver crafters is determined somewhat by the competition, but if your unique designs defy the competition, you have more freedom in setting your rate. The studio rate also depends on your skills and the popularity of your work. Silver crafters who work with sterling silver can typically establish a studio rate of $30 to $40 an hour. Those who silver plate can produce more products in an hour, but their studio rate is the same or slightly lower than for workers of genuine silver.

The key to fair prices is making your designs unique. If your silver jewelry uses precious stones, design interesting settings for them. Or mix other crafts with your silver (ceramics, fabrics, fine art, etc.) to make your products more distinctive. You need to get creative to get your price.

Gold Crafts

Many crafts rely on gold components to make them more attractive and more valuable. You may decide to work exclusively with gold or you may combine the precious metal with other crafts.

Gold is a soft metal so it doesn't naturally stand up to the wear that other metals can take. What is the allure of gold jewelry and crafts? It is a combination of the product's design and the impressive nature of the metal. People want to be known as someone who can appreciate and afford quality gold crafts. Gold is a vanity metal. There's nothing wrong with that, but you must remember to emphasize the total value of your products.

"This is a rich and elegant wrist bracelet that is a real attention-getter. Your friends will admire it."

Vanity costs more, too. The prices you can set for your gold jewelry and crafts will be higher because of the vanity factor. Some people find value in being able to say, "I paid eight hundred dollars for this piece."

Studio Rate

The studio rate for gold jewelers and crafters is higher than for related crafts. Experienced gold crafters can set an initial studio rate of $40 an hour or more and soon increase it to $50 or above, depending on demand. Remember, you want to price your crafts so that they are profitable. As noted in chapter one, if you're working too hard, increase your prices.

Exotic Metal Crafts

Silver and gold are not the only metals artisans use to craft. In fact, many crafters who previously worked in these metals have turned to more exotic metals for unique product ideas.

Exotic metals include nickel, brass, copper, pewter, iron and others. They are not really exotic metals, but they are exotic in crafting. Most craft shows will have relatively few booths selling copper or brass jewelry. Yet these metals offer as many opportunities for creativity and profit as precious metals. In addition, stock is less expensive. From these metals you can also produce candlesticks, coffee pots, kettles, pitchers, warming pans and related home products.

Studio Rate

The studio rate for crafting exotic metals depends on the crafter's skills and the tools required. However, because they are not vanity metals, exotic metals usually don't earn the crafter as high of a studio rate. The typical studio rates for exotic metals will range from $30 to $50 an hour, with most crafters in the bottom half of this range.

Gem Crafts

A wide variety of gems are processed and used in crafts today. A gem is a stone cut and polished for adornment. Some stones (diamonds, opals) are valuable or precious, while others are called semi-precious stones (topaz, garnet).

A crafter who cuts and polishes stones is called a lapidarist, and the craft is lapidary. Gem crafts are fine crafts requiring extensive skills and experience. These crafts can reward creative lapidarists with a good living if they develop their skills and find a profitable market.

Studio Rate

Depending on the level of skills and the crafter's reputation, the studio rate will range from $35 to $65 an hour. Lapidarists who are experts in preparing precious stones earn even more.

Hand Jewelry

Hand jewelry includes rings, wrist bracelets, ankle bracelets and related jewelry. Hand jewelry is quite popular, especially finger rings. Some jewel crafters specialize in rings—even in just one or two types of rings, such as children's rings. Specializing is necessary in a craft that has as much competition as hand jewelry. Make what you enjoy wearing or crafting.

Studio Rate

Creativity sets the studio rate for hand jewelry. Mass-producing simple designs will earn a studio rate of about $25 to $30 an hour. If you adapt common designs to create personalized variations, your studio rate will probably be about $5 to $10 an hour more. If you're making a few pieces of jewelry from your own designs, the typical studio rate rises to $45 to $55 an hour. Even higher rates are established by those designing and making one-of-a-kind hand jewelry.

Consider specializing in a specific stone or cut in your hand jewelry.

Neck Jewelry

Neck jewelry includes necklaces, neckchains, earrings, ear wires, bolo ties, crosses and related jewelry. Neck jewelry is typically worn to draw attention to the owner's face or neck. Therefore, the design should complement the owner's features without overpowering them. There's sometimes a fine line between the two.

Studio Rate

The studio rate for neck jewelry crafters is about the same or slightly lower than that for hand jewelers. Because the skills required to craft precious materials are usually more advanced jewelers who work with precious metals and stones typically charge a higher studio rate than those who work with less-costly materials. The risk factor of working with expensive materials is also greater.

Specifically, the studio rate for creative neck jewelry using precious materials is $35 to $65 an hour, depending on the the design and the skill of the crafter. Neck jewelry mass-produced from just a few designs earns a lower studio rate of $25 to $55 an hour.

Clothing Jewelry

Clothing jewelry includes lapel pins, hat pins, medallions, tie clips, broaches, watch fobs, belt buckles and similar jewelry. Some clothing jewelry serves a functional purpose as well as an esthetic one.

As with other jewelry and popular crafts, creativity pays. By simply revising a popular design to fit your own ideas of what the customer wants, you can increase the piece's perceived value and thus increase your price. For example, one creative clothing jeweler had seen so many cherub pins that she decided to create little devil pins. They soon caught on and she was making them of gold, silver and pewter, with some bejeweled. Each one was slightly modified from her basic design, making it relatively unique. Her hourly studio rate quickly moved from $30 to $55 because she was so busy. Once she saw the novelty of her devil pins wearing off, she sold her designs to a manufacturing company for mass production.

Forged Metals

Forged metal crafts are those that require the metal to be heated before it can be shaped. A blacksmith, for example, forges horseshoes, wrought iron railings and other metal products. Forging metals by hand is not a lost craft, but it is one that has been minimized by mechanization. Because forging metals is labor intensive, machines have replaced the efforts of crafters. And, frankly, the machines do a pretty good job.

How can you make money forging metal crafts? First, don't try to compete with machines. Find a specialty that is difficult to mechanize yet can be easily sold. Then learn all you can about your specialty to become an expert in the eyes of your customers. Build a reputation for creative designs and quality workmanship. Sell value.

Studio Rate

The studio rate for crafters working with forged metals is unfortunately on the lower end of the spectrum. It is typically within the range of $25 to $35 an hour for blacksmithing skills and slightly higher for crafts that require more creativity. Don't expect to get rich forging metals, but enjoying your craft can be its own reward.

Tinsmithing

Tin is a soft metal with a low melting point. Other than for lining cans, tin isn't used much today. Because most people associate tin with antiques, it is popular for antique reproductions such as kitchen utensils and cabinet doors.

Tin was an especially popular metal during the first 150 years of U.S. history. Tin was molded into candle molds, candlesticks, coffeepots, food warmers, plates, flour canisters, colanders, trays and other utensils. Some were formed by hand while others were manufactured.

Studio Rate

If you're a tinsmith or whitesmith, your skills will earn a studio rate similar to the blacksmith: $25 to $35 an hour and more for creativity. Tin products can be stenciled as reproductions of antique containers. Be creative; tin offers many possibilities.

Coppersmithing

Copper is another metal that was popular a century ago, but has been replaced by other metals and plastics in everyday life. Even so, working copper can be an interesting and rewarding craft. Especially if you concentrate your skills and creativity on one or two types of copper products.

Copper was once the metal of choice for kettles, cooking pots, warming pans, measuring cups and spoons, kitchen bowls, bed warmers and other day-to-day products. Copper is also an alloy in making brass (with zinc) and bronze (with tin).

If you have the skills and equipment to be a coppersmith, you can profitably produce and sell a variety of crafts. To determine whether the products you want to make are marketable, visit local and regional craft and antique shows. Search for others who will be your competitors and learn from them. In some cases, you can sell to them wholesale and thus not have to spend much time marketing your work. In other cases, you'll see a need for craft products that you can produce.

Studio Rates

The studio rate for coppersmithing is similar to other metal-working crafts, with the higher rates going to more creative efforts. Start out at $25 to $30 an hour until you're established; as described in chapter one, increase your studio rate as you get too busy.

Knives and Cutlery

A cutler makes, sells and/or repairs knives and other cutting instruments. This craft requires an extensive knowledge of many crafts. You must know metals. You must work with woods and other handle materials. You must especially develop the skill of metal sharpening. Sound like fun?

As a cutler, you must know your customer's needs well. You will be selling to chefs and others who consider their knives to be indispensable tools. Fortunately, because your customers make a living with knives and cutlery, they're more willing to pay for quality craftsmanship than the general public. By learning the customer's needs you can give them value and thus make a fair profit on your skills.

Studio Rate

Cutlers typically earn a slightly higher studio rate than other metal crafters because their skills must be more diverse. A cutler typically establishes a studio rate of $35 to $50 an hour, sometimes less if only sharpening customer's cutlery.

One successful cutler makes custom chef knives for professional chefs in northern California. By making a quality product and embossing his name on the wooden handles and knife racks, he promotes word-of-mouth advertising and is able to earn a shop rate on the high end of the scale: $50 an hour.

Other Metal Crafts

Working with metals can be among the most enjoyable crafts. You may decide to specialize in working with one metal, such as bronze, or in a product group, such as plated utensils. In each case, establishing a fair studio rate is vital to your success. If the rate is too high, you won't be able to sell your products. If the rate is too low, you won't be able to continue servicing your customers as you will be broke.

To set a fair studio rate for other metal or combined metal crafts, follow the guidelines in this chapter for those crafts closest to the one you select.

Remember, pricing is a craft that requires learning and experimentation.

CHAPTER SIX

How to Price Fine Arts

As a general rule, arts are sold in galleries and crafts through craft shows and related outlets, but the line between arts and crafts is indistinct. Artistic products may be sold at craft shows and fine crafts sold through art galleries.

Regardless of marketing venues, arts and crafts are priced in common. Artisans and crafters calculate material costs, estimate overhead, set a studio rate, ensure profit, and sell value. Artists don't need to be "starving" to sell their work.

Basics of Pricing Fine Arts

Art is a product of self-expression. Fine art is the manisfestation of this expression into things esthetically pleasing. The fine arts include painting, sculpture, drawing, watercolor, graphics and architecture.

In this chapter, we will discuss pencil drawing, pen and ink drawing, watercolors, oil painting, airbrush, portraits, caricature, calligraphy, photography, silhouette art, sculptures, painting on crafts and other artistic crafts.

One excellent source for marketing your fine arts is the annual *Artist's & Graphic Designer's Market* (Writer's Digest Books). It includes specific information on traditional artistic markets, such as galleries, as well as other opportunities to sell your art. It also includes information on artists' representatives, organizations and publications of value.

Costing Materials

Estimating the cost of your materials is important to accurate and profitable pricing. An artist's materials can vary in cost and quality as much as 500 percent for the same type of product. A part of the price difference is in quality, but some depends on how and where you buy the materials.

An excellent resource for buying artist's supplies is Margaret Boyd's book, *The Crafts Supply Sourcebook* (Betterway Books). It includes a section on sources of paints, finishes, adhesives, books, publications and associations. Another useful resource is *The Artist's Magazine* (F&W Publications), available on larger newsstands.

To develop an accurate cost of the materials used in fine arts, use the Materials Purchase Record and the Materials Use Record (see Appendix). It can help you determine the cost-per-item for your products, making pricing easier and ensuring profits. For example, track how much oil or watercolor paints you use in a typical painting; calculate the cost of mounted canvas by the square inch.

Estimating Overhead

What overhead expenses will you have as a fine artist? Of course, this depends on the fine art you follow. A photographer will have greater overhead expenses than a pencil artist. The Overhead Expenses worksheet (see Appendix) can help you estimate your overhead costs.

As you calculate overhead expenses, remember to estimate the cost of your studio—even if it's in your home. Use Internal Revenue Service form 8829, "Expenses for Business Use of Your Home," to figure your costs and deduction. The calculation will be based on the percentage of your home used for your fine arts business. Remember, if you receive more money than you spend, it's a business. You'll also need to file Schedule C, "Profit or Loss From Business."

Setting Studio Rates

How can an artist set a realistic studio rate for artistic talents and skills? This chapter includes typical studio rates (labor + overhead + profit) for a wide variety of fine arts based on interviews with artists and crafters. Use these suggested rates as a starting point for establishing your own studio rate based on your product, your skills and experience, local sales opportunities, and competition.

Fine artists usually have many years of experience and training in their art. Because of this, studio rates for fine artists are typically higher than those for most crafters. The average studio rate for fine artists ranges from $30 to $65 an hour, depending on skills and reputation. The studio rate for artists in demand can go to $100 or more an hour. As with crafts, these rates aren't based on leisurely hours of studying the model interspersed with watching TV. They are based on productive hours of efficient design and execution that are not hasteful or wasteful.

Ensuring Profit

Fine arts require both time and talents. To ensure that you get paid for both, make sure a realistic profit is built into your price.

As an example, a photographer sold his photos based on the cost of materials and studio rate. For a typical 8×10 photo, his materials cost $4, overhead was about $8 (including camera, lighting and darkroom equipment), his time was 1.5 hours at a studio rate of $40 an hour, and he set his profit margin at 10 percent. How much should he charge for this typical 8×10 photo?

	OF WHOLESALE	OF RETAIL
Materials	5%	2.5%
Overhead	10%	5.0%
Labor	75%	37.5%
Profit	10%	5.0%
Sales Costs		50.0%
Totals	100%	100%

Based on the above percentages, he should establish his wholesale price (to a gallery) at $80 and his retail price (at a fine arts fair) at $160. If he printed more than one copy of the negative and sold the prints, his production time goes up but the price per unit goes down. In addition, he may establish some negotiation component in his pricing, such as an additional 10 percent, to allow for those who must have a discount before deciding to buy.

Selling Value

How can you sell value with your fine arts? The most successful way is to build a name for yourself. Buyers of fine art don't just buy an object, they also buy the right to identify with the artist: "Yes, this is one of Josephine Smith's watercolors. She's quite popular in Santa Fe."

So how can you build your artistic name and value?

- Attend local and regional artists' parties.
- Work with local galleries and art fairs to promote your work and your name.
- Enter contests and win awards.
- Make sure the local newspapers know of any awards you win.
- Develop a distinctive signature for your fine art.

Help others see the artistic value of your creative talents and skills. Promote yourself. (For more ideas on marketing and self-promotion see chapter seven.)

You may eventually decide to use an agent to represent your artistic work. If so, check the Artists' Reps section of the annual *Artist's & Graphic Designer's Market* (Writer's Digest Books) for a listing of agents and representatives to the arts.

Pencil Drawing

Pencil drawing is a popular art that can express varied shades of beauty. As a fine art, it requires both craft and talent. Unfortunately, because pencil is perceived as a more temporary medium than others, its value is not as clearly identified by customers. Therefore, the studio rate for a pencil drawing is typically less than for other arts.

For example, a pencil drawing of a specific scene will typically sell for less than a watercolor or oil painting of the same scene even though the time and talents in both may be the same. To overcome this perception, some pencil artists use colors other than black. Others develop efficient drawing methods that help them produce quality art faster, thus increasing their studio rate. Still others simply accept the lower rate because pencil drawing is what they love.

Studio Rate

The studio rate for a pencil artist is typically in the range of $30 to $35 an hour depending on skills, experience and the medium. The salability of pencil drawings also depends on the subjects drawn. Some pencil artists specialize in regional or subject themes. One draws classic cars while another specializes in desert scenes with distant snow-capped mountains. Another concentrates her efforts in curbside portraits. Another uses charcoals rather than pencils for drawings.

Pen and Ink Drawing

Though the skills required of pen and ink artists are similar to those of pencil artists, they are sufficiently distinct to attract different buyers. The permanency of the medium requires the ink artist to work at a slower pace than the pencil artist. It is this permanency that allows ink artists to establish a slightly higher studio rate of $35 to $40 an hour.

As a pen and ink artist, what creative ways can you design, produce and market your skills? One successful artist did pen and ink drawings of large commercial booths at local trade shows, selling the rights of reproduction for the company's literature and advertisements. Many companies preferred a drawing rather than a photograph of their booth and were willing to pay for it. In many cases, the managers who could authorize the purchase were in the booth when the artist visited.

Watercolor Painting

The medium of water-based pigments or paints is one that draws many novice artists. Some artists stay with the medium, building their skills, while others move to oil-based pigments.

Studio Rate

The studio rate for typical watercolor painters is $35 to $40 an hour for experienced artists. Those new to the hobby often establish a rate $5 to $15 an hour lower, while those with advanced skills and training may add as much to the basic studio rate.

If you're an artist working in watercolors, look around at the work of other artists for a niche that you may enjoy and can easily sell. Nancy Ketterland produces watercolor paintings of historic homes in her region, selling prints through local galleries.

Oil Painting

The skills required to paint with oil-based pigments are perceived to be greater than those needed for watercolors. While this perception isn't true (the skills are *different*, rather than greater or lesser), the consumer still allows artists who work with oil paints a slightly higher studio rate.

Studio Rate

Advanced oil painters usually establish a basic studio rate of $40 to $50 an hour depending on many factors. These factors include experience, productivity, subject matter, originality of the art, popularity of the style, and the artist's name recognition. Some well-known oil painters have studio rates of $75 an hour or more.

Airbrush

Airbrush artistry is a technique for applying paints using an atomizer rather than a brush. Popular with automotive repainters and graphic artists, airbrush art has also moved into traditional art to create unique products with softer, blended colors. In most cases, airbrush art requires special paints and skills.

Studio Rate

The studio rate for an airbrush artist depends on the medium. Those who airbrush art on cars, trucks and recreational vehicles typically establish a studio rate of $35 to $55 an hour, depending on the popularity of the design and the skills of the artist. Other airbrush artists use a shop rate of $30 to $60 an hour, depending on the medium.

Portraits

Of course, portraits are a subject rather than a medium. Those who draw or paint portraits of individuals require advanced artistic skills and should be duly rewarded. An illustration of an apple doesn't have to look exactly like the subject apple, but the portrait of a living person must be realistic—or even a little kinder.

Studio Rate

Experienced portrait artists establish studio rates of $5 to $10 an hour above those typical of the medium. That is, a portrait artist working with watercolors may set a studio rate of $40 to $50 an hour ($35-$40 plus $5-$10). A portrait artist working in oil paints may set a studio rate of $45 to $60 an hour ($40-$50 plus $5-$10).

Are there popular locations in your community that make an ideal place to set up an easel on weekends to promote or even make create portraits?

Caricature

The art of drawing caricatures—illustrations emphasizing people's physical peculiarities—is a special talent. The drawing must be recognizable while accentuating unique features such as the subject's nose, ears, eyes, head shape or all of the above.

Studio Rate

Caricature drawings are typically done in pencil or in pen and ink, thus relying on the basic studio rate for these arts. But the talent of drawing caricatures adds value to the drawing and thus to the studio rate. As with portraits, the increased value should be at least $5 to $10 an hour. So caricatures done in pencil would use a studio rate of $35 to $45 an hour ($30-$35 plus $5-$10). Caricatures in ink would earn a studio rate of $40 to $50 an hour ($35-$40 plus $5-$10).

There's another factor to consider in the above studio rates: originality. The suggested studio rates are for unique, one-of-a-kind drawings. Your rate should be higher if your original design is reproduced for profit by you or others. That is, if you're drawing caricatures of famous people that will be used in a book or an advertisement, your studio rate should reflect the work's value to the client. Refer to the annual *Artist's & Graphic Designer's Market* (Writer's Digest Books) for specific rates of payment by publishers and advertising agencies.

Calligraphy

Calligraphy is the art of good penmanship. It has been a popular art form for hundreds of years, especially for religious and political documents. However, it has fallen in favor due to advancements in mechanized and computer typesetting. In moments, a desktop publishing system can produce documents that rival hours of work by a talented calligrapher.

Even so, those with advanced penmanship and calligraphic skills can apply them to a variety of products. One successful calligrapher works craft fairs and farmer's markets, offering personalized documents on-the-spot: wedding announcements, wedding vows, friendship scrolls and poems. Another successful calligrapher combined her skills with her knowledge of the German language to specialize in fraktur, an ornate calligraphy used by the Pennsylvania Germans. She reproduces geburts (birth certificates) and haus sagens (house blessings), selling them on special order at $40 to $65 each, depending on the size and time required. As you can imagine, she has little competition.

Studio Rate

The studio rate for a calligrapher is lower than for other fine arts—typically $25 to $35 an hour. However, a prolific and creative calligrapher can find ways of marketing more products by selling quality and value.

Photography

Photography is a fine art requiring tools, talents and tenacity. The photography of Ansel Adams, for example, elevated photography to an artistic form of beauty and emotion. Maybe you can do the same.

Studio Rate

The studio rate for an artistic photographer depends on talent as well as experience. The typical studio rate is $35 to $50 an hour, with the higher rates going to those who have developed a following.

The medium of photography allows artists to easily duplicate their finest works at low cost. A superlative photograph can be shared with many by simply making more copies in the darkroom. This feature allows the photographer to distribute the costs over more products. An outstanding photograph that required thirty hours of preparation can be copied and sold at a reasonable price to share its beauty with many; this system also makes the photographer's time investment financially worthwhile.

Elliott and Barbara Gordon's book, *How to Sell Your Photographs and Illustrations* (Allworth Press), offers additional ideas on pricing and marketing your photography.

Silhouette Art

To create or silhouette art, all you need is some black paper, some white paper, a pair of scissors, a subject and a tremendous amount of talent. Silhouette artists seen at craft fairs and other art functions have developed advanced skills of cutting silhouettes freehand. It's not as easy as it looks. Silhouette artists often begin their career cutting outlines of dogs, cats, mountains and other subjects in their studio where people aren't watching every cut made. Their skills progress toward freehand silhouettes.

Studio Rate

Freehand silhouette skills can earn a silhouette artist $40 to $60 an hour. Until then, studio silhouette artists establish a typical rate of $25 to $35 an hour, depending on skills and experience.

Bob Hamilton works the craft fairs producing on-the-spot silhouette art. Bob also offers a variety of frames made by his wife to his customers. The combined art and craft earn them a very good supplemental income for a few hours of "fun."

Sculptures

Sculpture is three-dimensional art. Sculptured mediums include formed clay, carved wood, chiseled stone, molded plaster, welded steel and iron and other shaped materials. Each requires its own unique talents and skills.

Studio Rate

The studio rate for sculptors depends much on the market for the medium and the reputation of the artist. A beginning sculptor working with common materials may have difficulty establishing a studio rate of $35 an hour, while an experienced marble sculptor may have a rate twice that figure.

How can you set your most efficient studio rate? First, study your competitors and the prices of their completed works. This may require some travel to distant shows if your medium is unique or you live in a rural area. Second, estimate the time it would take you to produce a similar sculpture, then deduct the cost of materials. From these figures, calculate the studio rate you would need to sell a similar sculpture for the competitor's price. Make sure you use the wholesale price (retail minus marketing costs).

Painting on Crafts

Some artists specialize in adding creative artistry to crafts. They paint scenes or portraits on craft products they or others have produced. They add a design to a friend's ceramics or to their own metal crafts. How can they establish fair pricing on products that combine art and craft? Separately.

For example, one artist paints delicate flowers on her husband's china blanks before they are fired. Because of skills and experience, he has set a studio rate of $35 an hour for his ceramics. She adds the flower designs at a studio rate of $45 an hour. Both studio rates will contribute to the final price.

Another related craft is theorem, the creation of multicolored art using stencils, one for each color. It was popular during the first half-century of America's history and is again popular with those reproducing period art from that era. Theorem is typically done with watercolors on furniture or paper.

Other Artistic Crafts

There are many other artistic crafts. Some are nearly forgotten arts that are beginning a resurgence, while others are based on popular arts or newer technologies. How can you efficiently price other artistic crafts?

First, compare the art to more established or popular arts and their typical studio rates. Second, modify the rate based on relative ease or complexity, increasing or decreasing the studio rate as appropriate. Third, look for ways of increasing productivity and thus maintaining a higher studio rate. Finally, modify your studio rate to reflect the customer's perception of value.

Approach pricing as a craft that can be learned through study, analysis and practice. It can also be fun.

CHAPTER SEVEN

How to Increase Profits Without Reducing Quality

Congratulations! By now you've probably started making money selling your crafts at fair prices. If not, you're on the way. This final chapter offers creative ideas on:

1. How to sell more of your crafts
   - Learn to sell smart at craft shows and other sales outlets
   - Consider consignment selling
   - Hire a sales representative
   - Sell by mail
   - Go after commissioned work
2. How to keep more of what you earn
   - Keep accurate records
   - Estimate your craft's break-even point
   - Manage cash flow
   - Learn how and when to increase prices
   - Use outsourcing to your advantage
   - Stay out of business traps
   - Get valuable business advice for free
   - Learn how to pay minimal taxes

These and related topics—all with the objective of increasing profits without reducing quality—will be covered in this comprehensive chapter.

Selling at Craft Shows

The largest sales opportunity for crafters is often craft shows and outdoor art festivals. There are hundreds across the nation every weekend. Larger ones have attendance of up to a half-million people, but most fairs draw a few thousand potential buyers.

Depending on your specialty, you may sell some of your craft projects at craft shows and fairs. Selling through craft fairs requires that you spend as much as half of your time preparing for or attending shows. Retail craft shows typically estimate an average sale of between $30 and $60, depending on size and publicity.

The cost of a booth (or perhaps more accurately, booth *space* because at most shows you will have to provide your own display materials—tables, shelves, signage, etc.) at a craft show, fair or festival ranges from $25 to as much as $150 per booth for a weekend. Regional and national show fees are higher and may include a percentage of your sales.

Some show managers will allow you to rent a booth for a single day if you wish. If you rent the booth for a two-day weekend, your agreement will probably require that you have someone at the show for all show hours unless another arrangement is made. Most shows are open from about 10 A.M. to 5 P.M., depending on the type of show, the theme of the show (holiday, event, year-round, etc.) and local customs. Many shows don't open on Sunday until after 12 P.M. to allow for church attendance.

As you exhibit at craft shows and keep good sales records you will soon determine how many sales you can expect per thousand people in attendence. You may find that you sell 1.4 quilts, for example, for every thousand attendees. Or it may be 3.2 charcoal portraits per thousand. With this ratio you can better determine whether a specific craft show will be worth your time and efforts. By estimating costs to attend the show, calculating the value of your time, and dividing that amount by projected sales, you can estimate the profitability of a specific show. Of course, much depends on your location at the show, the show hours, how many of your competitors are there, the weather and many other factors beyond your control.

Besides retail craft shows and fairs, you can choose to sell your craft products at festivals, mall shows and exhibits. Other successful crafters rent space in a permanent or seasonal craft mall in a tourist area.

Booth Design

Before designing your craft booth, visit craft shows at which you expect to exhibit. Find the "Information Booth" and get an exhibitor's package with information on booth size, requirements and limitations. Standard booth size ranges from $8' \times 10'$ to $10' \times 10'$. Plan your booth so it can be easily modified for various widths and depths without reducing its effectiveness.

As you visit potential craft shows, look at your competitors' booths. How do they encourage people to stop? Is their booth open, inviting people to step in, or is it closed to allow more room for storing stock? What booth, in your opinion, has the most effective design? Which one has the most people stopping and buying? How does the booth get people to stop? Does it use banners, large signs, sample crafts, display tables or something else? Are prices clearly marked, or do customers have to ask? Apply your creative skills to improving on the best ideas from each show. Design your booth so new ideas can easily be incorporated into its design without major changes.

Develop a Mailing List

Depending on your craft products, you may want to encourage people who attend craft shows to sign up for your mailing list. In fact, if you sell higher-priced craft products, you may find that most of your sales will come from customers who are introduced to you at the shows but don't buy until a relationship is built through direct mail and even telephone contacts. Craft shows become opportunities to show your product and *begin* the selling process. You will finalize sales at your showroom or studio.

To develop a mailing list, leave a sign-up sheet in your booth for a free newsletter or brochure. Some crafters offer seasonal discounts to customers on their mailing list. Others send quarterly letters to their mailing list telling customers about shows they will be attending and, if available, offering discount or complimentary tickets to the show.

Know Your Market

Remember to dress the part. That is, if you're selling country quilts, dress up like a country quiltmaker. If you make and sell Shaker reproductions, wear clothing that looks like it comes from that period. It may be just a shirt or shawl or a hat. Even your wearing a studio apron helps customers feel like they are buying from an artisan.

Craft shows will also help you determine what doesn't sell. That is, you may want to sell handmade gold jewelry at craft shows but notice, at shows in your region, gold jewelry doesn't sell well enough to cover show expenses. You can consider developing a more novel way of selling smaller pieces at shows—or you can decide to sell them another way. As you walk the shows, keep a notebook on your observations. Also talk with both exhibitors and attendees to find out what works and what doesn't. You may learn from the trials of an experienced craft show exhibitor without having to pay for their mistakes. You'll get a low-cost education that can save you hundreds of dollars and many hours of frustration.

Woodcrafter Nancy Bartow makes a variety of woodcraft gift items and sells them at art and craft fairs throughout the Pacific Northwest. All of her items are under $50 each, and most are priced between $15 and $20 each. She prices her work based on time and materials as well as a comparison with the competition. Nancy said, "We've added and dropped many items over the years because we could not competitively sell them and still make money." She knows her customers well, spending many weekends in her booth talking with craft show buyers.

Resources

How can you find out what shows are in your area? Ask other crafters, ask at local craft supply stores, watch local newspapers, contact area chambers of commerce and subscribe to craft magazines that list regional shows. *Sunshine Artists* magazine (800) 597-2573 lists hundreds of announcements each month. You should also consider subscribing to *The Crafts Report* (P.O. Box 1992, Wilmington, DE 19899; (800) 777-7098. *The Crafts Report* estimates that craft sales add about $300 million a year to the national economy. It's an excellent publication for those in the business of making and selling crafts. It also includes information on shops and galleries looking for crafts. In addition, the American Craft Council sponsors craft marketing events each year in major cities, produced by American Craft Enterprises (21 S. Eltings Corner Rd., Highland, NY 12528; (800) 836-3470). These events are about 75 percent wholesale and 25 percent retail.

Use the sample Show Travel Expense Report form in the appendix of this book to better track the costs of selling at shows.

Selling at Flea Markets

So-called flea markets can be lucrative sales opportunities for crafters. On any given weekend, thousands of flea markets are in progress across the nation. Some specialize, but most offer everything from home-grown herbs to handmade potholders. Here are some ideas on how you can improve your sales through flea markets.

Choosing Your Market and Your Site

First, select a flea market that draws a consistently large crowd, but not so large that it is difficult to manage. When considering a flea market, ask the promoter how many square feet of floor space you will get, the dimensions of the space, the location of the space, what tables or covers the promoter will furnish, what other merchants will be located near your booth, where the primary traffic pattern is and the hours of the show.

Second, make sure there is a good mix of vendors and, if possible, select a site near vendors of similar products. Don't worry about competition; let them worry about you. Make a good and useful product, price it fairly and sell its value, and you won't have any competition.

Third, be consistent. A flea market attendee may see your booth many times before buying from you. So long as it is profitable, have a booth at the flea market every week. If possible, set up your booth at the same site every time. If you can't, make sure your booth is recognizable from a distance with a large sign or signature decoration.

Fourth, make sure that your booth is attractive and encourages buyers to stop and look. Use your creative skills to make a handsome booth. Look at the booths of other vendors and select the best elements from many to incorporate into your design. Of course, also make sure that it is a booth that can be set up in less than an hour and easily stored during the off-season.

Fifth, have something for everyone. If you are selling large craft products, have a few small items to sell, or even to give away. You can offer smaller versions of your primary crafts or related products. If possible, offer items starting at just a few dollars for those who want something you've made, even though they can't afford your primary product. Remember most people who come to a flea market are "just browsing" and you must have some lower-priced products for them to take home.

Finally, have fun. Talk with prospective customers. Use the opportunity to do market research, pricing research and to understand what buyers are looking for.

The Great American Flea Market Directory (P.O. Box 543, Fenton, MO 63026) lists the names, locations and dates for hundreds of flea markets and swap meets across the nation.

Selling Your Crafts to Retailers

Thus far, this book has primarily discussed selling your own craft projects. Of course there are many other ways to sell what you make. Most crafters start by selling their own work, so they learn directly from the customer what sells and what doesn't. They develop invaluable knowledge of their market and their craft. Later, because of time limits or preferences, they often sell their products to retailers who then sell to the general public.

The largest retail market for smaller craft products—leaded glass, tole painting, jewelry, ceramics and the like—is gift shops and craft shops. There are nearly 70,000 gift shops in the U.S. and another 8,000 in Canada. In addition, there are over 3,000 arts-and-craft shops in the U.S. and about 500 in Canada. Together they make up a tremendous opportunity to sell smaller craft products with a retail price of under $150. Craft products must be small because they require shipment, an expense that can take much of the profit of a larger, lower-priced item.

Depending on your craft, also consider selling through museum gift shops, church bazaars and mall kiosks and pushcarts operated by others.

Contacting Craft Shops

A proven way to sell to gift and craft shops is to contact them direct. A recent survey of craft shops conducted by *Woodshop News* reports that 91 percent will purchase directly from a crafter who contacts them; 44 percent prefer a letter; 30 percent prefer to talk with the craftsperson by phone; and 24 percent accept unannounced visits, as long as it's not at a normally busy time.

You'll find the names and addresses of gift and craft shops in telephone book yellow pages. You can also purchase a mailing list of shops in your state or region. The lists are typically typed labels that you can affix to your brochure or sales package. Mailing lists are available through list brokers and mailing services (see metropolitan or business-to-business phone books) for about $.10 a name in quantity.

Do a little market research. Make sure that the craft and gift shops you approach purchase items similar to what you make and in the price range of your work. That is, don't try to sell $1,500 gold necklaces to a country craft store, to such a store you would sell antiqued lapel pins or similar items. How can you learn what a shop prefers to sell? Call or visit them.

Wholesale Craft Shows

Some crafters prefer to show their products at wholesale craft shows and sell directly to retailers. The purpose of the show is to give you an opportunity to present your products to as many retailers as possible and to take advance orders. According to a recent survey by *Woodshop News*, 81 percent of the craft retailers interviewed go to these shows. Over one-half of all their purchases are made at wholesale shows. This is, obviously, an excellent way for you to meet buyers.

Other Retail Opportunities

If you're making unique works of art with high price tags—oil paintings, hand-carved murals, fine hand-painted ceramics, etc.—offer your works to art galleries and dealers. There are about 22,000 galleries in the U.S. and another 3,200 in Canada. You'll command a higher price for unique craft products, but you'll sell fewer.

Antique craft reproductions often sell best at antique stores. There are more than 34,000 antique dealers in the U.S. and about 2,500 in Canada. Mailing list brokers can give you a list of them by state, by region and even by specialty: originals, reproductions, kitchen utensils only, etc.

Some craft products require creativity in selling as well as making. For example, handmade tapestries can be sold in art galleries, gift shops, museum shops and even upscale restaurants. Hand-painted china can be sold to restaurant supply wholesalers who sell them to fine restaurants. Or you can sell portraits of a large corporation's founders and executives for display in its lobby.

Pricing Guidelines

One gallery owner told me that some crafters are upset when they hear that the gallery will sell the craft product for twice what the shop pays for it. For example, a painting for which the artist receives $500 is retail priced at $1,000. Why does the gallery get so much? The owner explains, of the retail price, 50 percent goes to the artist, about 20 percent goes for overhead to run the gallery, and another 20 percent pays for the gallery staff. That leaves the gallery a 10 percent profit before taxes. If the shop owner must give a 10 percent discount to a good customer or put the item on sale, the profit is gone.

An extensive list of galleries, by state, is included in *Artist's & Graphic Designer's Market* (Writer's Digest Books).

As a guideline, expect to sell your craft products to retailers at about 50 percent of the retail price (the price at which they expect to sell it). That is, they will typically pay about $150 wholesale for a craft they expect to sell retail at $295. Set your wholesale prices accordingly. If you determine the production cost of your craft is $180, you may want to set a wholesale price of $200 and suggest the retail price of $395.

Offering Credit

Should you offer terms to retail stores? Much depends on whether your business has sufficient funds to cover the problems that credit can give you. Offering credit terms—based on payment plans of thirty, sixty or ninety days—instead of cash on delivery can increase your sales, but it can also increase your headaches. Still, most businesses believe—and profit from— the philosophy of increasing profits through managed credit. That is, as long as you carefully manage credit and to whom you give it, you will come out ahead. If you want to keep your craft venture small and feel you have sufficient customers to do so, then terms can be cash with order or cash on delivery (COD). But if you're trying to build a part-time business where others have already gone, you may want to offer credit terms to encourage retailers to buy from you. Many craftspeople will insist on cash while they are starting their business, then add credit terms when they are ready to expand. The appendix of this book includes a typical credit application that you can photocopy and use.

Frame maker Rick Rochon of Olor Enterprises offers three credit terms:

cash with order, COD or on account. His shipper will collect on delivery for a small fee, which Rick tacks on to the price of the order. In establishing an account, Rick requires three credit references. He may or may not verify the references, depending on the size of the first order. His theory is: "Who would give me a bad credit reference?"

Nontraditional Avenues for Displaying Your Crafts

Depending on your craft, you can display samples at nontraditional retail and service businesses. For example, you can ask your banker to display your paintings in their lobby or on a counter. Or you can suggest that they promote the local arts and purchase some of your craft products for their office or as gifts to their best customers. Another excellent location to display or sell your work is at area restaurants. Family restaurants may appreciate having art or old-fashioned decorations in their waiting area.

As you contact these businesses, ask for the owner or manager, explain that you are a local crafter, and suggest specific products that would look good in their business. Ask if the business would buy some of your products. If not, can you display them there?

Other locations where you may be able to sell or display your craft products include: attorney, accountant, doctor and other professional offices; libraries; corporate offices and municipal buildings.

Consignment Selling

Selling wholesale to retail stores is a popular alternative to sitting at a craft show all weekend. Finding retail outlets for your craft products can make life much easier. However, while some retailers will pay in advance or within thirty days of delivery, others will want your products on consignment. Should you agree to these terms? It depends.

Twenty-seven percent of all craft studios surveyed by *Woodshop News* report that they carry most of their work on consignment. Another 19 percent take some crafts on consignment—mostly larger pieces—and purchase the rest.

How Consignment Works

Under a typical consignment deal, you let the retailer display your product without buying it. They only pay you when they sell the product. Consignment shops typically pay from 50 to 70 percent of retail. That is, if they sell your $100 craft product, they will pay you between $50 and $70. As an average, they will pay you about two-thirds of the retail price and keep one-third for their efforts. You earn an extra 17 percent of the retail price (34 percent of the wholesale price). You also take the risk that the product won't sell or, if sold, the retailer won't pay you as promised. Some crafters simply increase their wholesale prices to compensate for the risk. Others limit their consignments to a percentage of all sales. Some will offer products on consignment only to outlets that they want to develop as primary customers. Still other crafters refuse to sell any products on consignment.

Recordkeeping Is Important

Consignment selling is more common with artistic products sold through art dealers or galleries, but can be used to sell any type of craft product. It requires that you keep accurate and complete records on every piece you consign, that you require a signature on delivery, and that you set a time limit on the consignment. Some merchants will move consignment pieces to the back room if they don't sell quickly. They want to first sell the products they have purchased. A typical consignment period is 90 to 180 days.

Other Options

But what if you don't want to sell on consignment and the store doesn't want to buy it for cash? You have some alternatives. You can require cash on delivery but offer a return policy if it hasn't sold within 90 to 180 days. Of course, you will have to carefully watch your checkbook as the return of a large shipment can take the balance down fast. You can also offer your first sale to a new customer on consignment, but require that reorders be on cash or 30-day terms.

Using a Sales Representative or Distributor

The job of a sales representative is to trade some of your headaches for some of your money. He or she can take over the task of selling what you make and give you time to make more. It can be a good investment or an even bigger headache.

A sales representative might be your exclusive sales agent, or sell only in a specific region of the country, or sell only a few of your products. It's up to you. Some crafters find sales reps for regions of the country that they can't cover. Then, as business grows, they offer their local region as a sales territory to the same or another sales representative.

Paying the Sales Rep

How much should you pay a sales rep? That depends on what the rep does for you. Some will spend much time representing you at wholesale shows, taking your products into retail stores, sending out brochures and price lists (see appendix), and making sure your products are being displayed well. Others will throw a couple of your samples in their bag as they travel from store to store. Most reps are paid by commission, a percentage of what they sell. The exact percentage depends on what they do to earn the sale and at what price they sell the product. It may also depend on the volume they sell during a given period. Commissions may change as sales volume changes. One sales rep may receive only 5 percent commission of retail price. Another may earn as much as 30 percent of retail for his or her efforts. A typical sales commission is in the middle: 10 to 20 percent of retail. However, your cost might be little or nothing the rep receives a higher wholesale price for your craft products.

Distributors vs. Sales Reps

A distributor is similar to a rep in that they both sell your craft products. Distributors take on some marketing responsibilities and sometimes warehouse a product they sell, as well. For this, the typical distributor gets 35 percent commission.

How can you find a sales representative or distributor? Contact Rep

Registry (P.O. Box 2306, Capistrano Beach, CA 92624), look for rep ads in your craft magazines or ask other crafters.

Selling by Mail

Many crafters have successfully sold their products by mail. Shipping costs can limit the size of craft products sold by mail, but the primary factor of limitation is often price. The cost-per-sale can be $5 to $50 depending on the item, so the product is usually not an $8 item. If it is, it should be one that will encourage customers to buy more from the seller. On the other end, it is difficult to sell products for over about $100 by mail unless the firm's reputation has been built to the level of an L.L. Bean or a J.C. Penney.

One successful crafter lives on the Oregon coast, yet sells his products across the nation. He depends extensively on shipping services to allow him to deliver his products anywhere in just a few days of an order. "I sell very few of my products locally. If it weren't for UPS I'd be out of business." He established an account with major shipping services and set up a shipping table in his shop. Each day the drivers stop by to pick up any outgoing packages.

Direct-Mail Marketing

Craftspeople who sell by mail use printed postcards, brochures or minicatalogs to send information on their products to prospective customers. A crafter can produce a four-color catalog sheet for about $500 and mail it to craft stores, gift shops, retail stores or directly to prospective customers. Depending on the quality of the list, about 2 percent of the recipients will order.

Mail-order sales campaigns can get quite expensive. If you plan to use this method of selling your craft, look for a direct-mail consultant who will help you develop a profitable campaign. A consultant will charge a fee, but will typically save sufficient postage or earn you sufficient sales to cover the costs. However, most direct mail consultants won't work on campaigns smaller than a few thousand dollars in total cost. You can also hire a freelance copywriter to help create the promotional piece. The alternative is to learn as much as you can about direct mail and copywriting, then design your own mail-order system for selling your craft products.

Another alternative is to cooperate with noncompeting crafters in a direct-mail campaign and split the costs. You may even find crafters in your group that have direct-mail or mail-order experience.

Product Dealers

Crafters can also sell their products by mail through mail-order product dealers. The dealer may specialize in gift items or personalized items. Approach them as you would a retail outlet with samples and ideas. Some mail-order outlets will require that you be able to produce a specific number of units within a short time, so be ready to do so if you want their order. They don't want to sell two thousand of your needlecraft products if you can only produce four a day.

Shipping Your Product

If you decide to develop a mail-order business, do some research to find the best way of shipping your products to customers. Depending on what you sell, to whom, and where they are located, you may select the postal service, a package delivery service, an overnight service or even a freight service. Check your area phone books under "Delivery Service," "Shipping" or "Mailing Services." If you live in a rural area or most of your customers do, you may be limited in the delivery services offered. Even so, any service you select will help you determine how best to package and ship your products for safe arrival in a timely manner. The appendix of this book includes typical shipping forms (invoice, packing slip and shipping labels) you can photocopy for your own use.

For More Information

Maria Piscopo's book, *Marketing and Promoting Your Work* (North Light Books), includes more detailed suggestions on how to make good use of direct mail in selling your crafts. My book, *The Upstart Guide to Owning and Managing a Mail Order Business*, offers extensive resources on this topic. For more information on mail-order sales, contact the Direct Marketing Association (6 E. 43rd St., New York, NY 10017).

Selling Commissioned Crafts

A commission is an agreement to execute an idea. The idea can be yours or your client's. Some crafters find their niche here, at the high end. They sell their craft products to those who will pay for unique artistry purchased directly from the artist. Their clients are large corporations, corporate executives, foundations, art connoisseurs, art patrons, museums and public art galleries. Each piece is designed for and commissioned by the particular client.

Besides the money, a commissioned work can enhance a crafter's or artist's reputation. Photos of a commissioned work can be used to promote your artistic or craft services.

Studio Rate

The studio rate for commissioned art is higher than for other crafts—often between $50 and $100 an hour—but so is the risk. Artisans who sell commissioned work typically have a tested system for establishing and collecting fees. They have developed business experience, have sold other works, have earned name recognition through awards, and have a contract requiring deposits and payments. Few crafters start at this level, but most aspire to it.

Commissioned craft projects are typically paid for in two installments. The first installment should be made when the commission is accepted and the project is outlined. A letter from you to the purchaser describing the project and the payment terms can serve as a basic contract. Depending on the size of the project, the length of time required, and your negotiating skills, you may receive the second installment at a specific point in the project or when the project is delivered. Some crafters establish a three-payment plan to help with their own cash flow.

If you're selling commissioned art or crafts, speak with a lawyer about developing a simple agreement that will ensure that you get paid.

Becoming a Business

Once you have a taste of profitably selling your crafts, you may decide to make it a part-time or even full-time business. This chapter offers many suggestions and resources for starting a business. Remember: If you just spend money on it, it's a hobby. If you can make money on it, it's a business.

Get a Business Phone

Many of the successful crafters interviewed for this book said that a separate business telephone is a necessity, especially if you have teenagers or other excessive phone users in the family. You will also need an answering system, particularly if your business is a part-time venture. You could be losing half of your business by not having a professional and efficient phone system. If others will be answering the phone, suggest they use the sample Phone Message form in the appendix of this book to help ensure that you get important messages.

If you will be answering the phone with a business name rather than a personal name, you need a business line. If your name is Mary Jones and your firm is "Mary Jones Leathercraft," you can answer "Mary Jones" and not confuse your prospects and clients. But if you're "Quality Leathercrafts" and you answer "Mary Jones," some callers may think they have the wrong number. The cost of a business line has decreased over the last few years because of the competition among telephone companies, so it is a more affordable business investment.

Answering Systems

Not long ago, an answering machine was an annoying and misused tape recorder that attempted to drive off the people who called you. Today's answering machine is much more accepted, especially in business. It's also easier to use and cheaper to buy.

A good answering machine for business use should include a feature that voice-prints the day and time of incoming calls, should give you the ability to check and change messages from remote locations, and should not limite the length of incoming messages.

Unfortunately, many businesses misuse their answering system by putting cryptic announcements and background music on the system that confuse or intimidate callers. An effective message should be something like:

"Hello, this is Quality Leathercraft's answering system. Your call is important to us. Please leave your name and telephone number after the beep and someone will get back to you as soon as possible. Or, if you'd prefer, please call again later. Thank you."

If you want your business to be successful, it must sound successful.

Additional information on the business side of your craft is available in Kathryn Caputo's book, *How to Start Making Money with Your Crafts*, Barbara Brabec's popular *Homemade Money* and Jo Frohbieter-Mueller's *Stay Home and Mind Your Own Business*, all published by Betterway Books.

Keeping Good Records

Most craftspeople dislike keeping records, even though they understand the necessity. Profit is whatever is left in the wallet at the end of the month. Estimated taxes are always underestimated. A budget is what they'll set up next year.

Your recordkeeping system doesn't have to be complex to set up or painful to use. You need to keep track of only a few things: how much you receive and how much you spend. You can make your job easier by keeping more detailed records, but they aren't necessary.

The appendix of this book includes Craft Sales Record and Cash Receipts worksheets for recording money you receive and a Cash Disbursements worksheet for recording money you spend. These forms can be customized and copied for your craft business.

If you prefer, an office supply stationery, or large discount store will have bound books of lined paper with two columns (a "journal") for less than $5 each. Label the first column "Income" and the second "Expenses." On each line, write the date, whom you received money from or paid money to, and the amount of money exchanged in the appropriate column. At the end of each page write "Balance Forward," total the columns, and copy the "Balances" to the first line of the next page. With this system, you can determine your current income and expenses at any time. Subtract expenses from income and that figure is your profit (or loss).

Some crafters use the front of their journal for recording their checkbook entries and pages in the back for keeping track of cash payments. For record-keeping purposes, use a check for most of what you buy. However, sometimes you don't want to write a check for a skein of yarn or a packet of sandpaper and you pay cash. Keep the receipt. Keep track of these small cash payments.

Once a month or whenever they total more than about $50, write a check to yourself for the total of all these business receipts. As your hobby becomes a business it becomes more important to separate your personal money from that of your business.

Tracking Jobs and Time

How can you keep track of the time you spend on projects? There are many ways. The simplest is to write down everything in one location: a wall calendar, a day planner or a bound "Record" book from the same source as your journal. Everything is in one place. It may be disorganized, but it's there. A better method is to keep separate records of each job you're doing, either in file folders or in a three-ring binder. Some crafters do both; they have a project file and a calendar to write personal notes.

To make the task of keeping time records easier, the appendix of this book includes Things To Do and Monthly Planner forms that you can copy and customize. You can also buy a variety of planners that include task lists as well as other features, such as hourly, daily, weekly and monthly scheduling.

Using a Spreadsheet

If you have a computer that you can use for your business records, invest in a spreadsheet or checkbook program. You can purchase a basic spreadsheet program for about a hundred dollars that will let you enter rows or lines of job expense names (Labor, Materials, etc.) and columns of numbers. Most important, you can then tell the program to total any or all of the columns or rows and it will do so in less than a second. If you update a number, it automatically recalculates the total for you.

Fancier and more costly spreadsheets and checkbook programs can follow your instructions, *macros*, to do special calculations automatically. You could, for example, write a macro that will select all of the invoices over sixty days old and total them. Better spreadsheet and checkbook programs will also produce fancy graphs and pie charts that impress lenders and other financial types.

Estimating Craft Break-Even Points

A simple calculation called the break-even point can help you make your craft venture more profitable. The break-even point is the point at which income equals expenses. For example, if you're selling silver necklaces at $75 each and you need $900 each month to cover expenses and wages for your part-time venture, your break-even point is twelve units. If you sell eighteen units that month, you've made a healthy profit. If you only sold ten units, you've lost money.

Calculated Fixed and Variable Costs

To estimate your break-even point you need to add up all of your fixed costs (wages, rent, equipment, etc.) and variable costs (materials, etc.). A fixed cost is one that goes on whether you sell anything or not. A variable cost changes as you make and sell products. Adding these two costs together tells you how much you need to make each month. Divide this by the amount you will receive for a typical product. If you make many craft products, you may have a number of break-even points depending on which products you sell. In the above example, you may need to sell eighteen small necklaces or nine large ones to break even each month. If you usually sell four small necklaces for every one large unit, you need to sell about twelve small units and three large units each month.

Knowing your craft business's break-even point can help you decide whether to concentrate more on marketing or on production that month. It can help you stay profitable.

Managing Your Cash

One of the biggest complaints heard from business owners is that money doesn't come in as fast as it must go out. Even though there are more sales dollars than expense dollars, making those sales dollars arrive on time can be a big headache. Your craft enterprise will be no exception.

How do large businesses tackle this headache? They manage their cash flow. They keep track of not only sales, but when sales will turn into income. That is, if you've sold twelve craft products to a wholesaler at $110 each, you have a sale of $1320, but maybe no income for thirty, sixty, or ninety days or more. What do you do in the meantime to buy needed materials, make equipment repairs, and pay for shipping costs?

Projecting Income

One option is to require payments on specific dates with a late fee for missing those dates. This option enables you to project when you will get income and make plans accordingly. You will then write those expected payments on a cash flow projection or forecast. You will include other time payments to get a clearer picture of when sales dollars will become income dollars. The appendix of this book includes a blank Cash Flow Forecast form for your use.

Another option for improving cash flow is to set a firm credit policy and stick to it. Your policy may be any of the following:

- Cash or local check on delivery
- Cash, check or credit card
- Net 30 days
- 2/10, net 30

Many businesses offer the terms: 2/10; net 30. That means the customer gets a 2 percent discount if they pay within 10 days, but the net invoice amount is due and payable within 30 days.

Credit Card Sales

Accepting credit cards will definitely increase your sales to retail customers. In fact, one study indicated increases of an average of 38 percent in business due to credit card sales. Many people are more inclined to buy if they can put it on their Visa, MasterCard or Discover card. How can you help them buy? Chances are, until your craft business grows, you will not be able to get your bank to set you up as a credit card merchant. Besides, doing so is expensive; you need specific equipment and you must pay a fee of 2 to 4 percent on each transaction. You may be able to lease the equipment, but costs per transaction are still high if you don't sell a minimum amount on charge cards.

There is an alternative: Some banks will allow you to take transactions on charge cards without being a card merchant. They give you the required forms and instructions, which you fill out for the customer and return to the bank. The bank then processes the transaction for you. There will be an additional transaction fee, but it can save you the expenses of purchasing transaction equipment you will rarely use. This option allows you to offer charge cards as a payment option—and improve your cash flow—without a major investment. If this sounds right for you, talk with your banker.

In any case, beware of offers from firms that will get you credit merchant status for an up-front fee. Some are reputable, but too many are not. In some cases, the fees are exorbitant or they don't do what they promise. A small business cannot afford to make $1,000 mistakes very often. Play it safe and work with your bank or a trusted trade association if you want to offer payment by credit card. Check your local library for a reference book called the *Encyclopedia of Associations* (Gale Research) for a comprehensive listing of business and consumer associations.

Sometimes you can use a craft guild or trade association to help you gain credit card merchant status. You can find a comprehensive listing of craft and artist associations in *Artist's & Graphic Designer's Market* (Writer's Digest Books).

Increasing Your Prices

As your craft venture grows, you have two options:
1. Make more product
2. Make more money

For many part-time craft ventures, the first action is to make more product. That is, the part-time weaving venture becomes a full-time business. This may be exactly what you want to do—or it may not. You may prefer to do your craft on a part-time basis, making a profit but not giving up what you do the rest of the time, whether it be working a full-time job, golfing or spending time with your family.

In this case, you have a second option: Make more money. You can do so by increasing your studio rate; you might decide to go from $30 an hour to $35 an hour for all products you make after a specific date. Or you can increase your profit margin. You can also maintain your studio rate but try for a higher wholesale or retail price.

Don't Sell Yourself Short

Remember, too many craftspeople sell their talents short; they underprice their work and they undervalue their skills. Learn to realistically price your craft projects so you can continue to do what you love.

To increase your prices, decide what your new pricing should be, calculate how it will impact your unit prices, set a date for the increase and then be flexible.

One successful crafter built most of his products on the weekends, primarily on Saturday to allow Sunday for family. About a year after he began, he found himself working at least ten hours on Saturday and four on Sunday—and still getting behind on orders. He had a potential contract with a hardware retailer that, combined with his other business, could give him a total of twenty-five hours of work a week. He could almost take his craft venture into a full-time business.

Instead, the crafter decided not to bid on the hardware contract until he had more business experience. Rather, he decided to increase his studio rate by 25 percent—from an hourly rate of $32 to $40. Because most of his sales were directly to the customers and labor was one-half of his price, his retail prices increased 12.5 percent. An $80 craft product became $90. This change didn't reduce his sales, but gave him the funds to employ his teenage daughter on Saturdays as a shop assistant. He was back to one weekend workday and had the chance to spend it with a member of his family. After his daughter's graduation—if she still enjoys the craft—this smart crafter plans to bid on wholesale jobs to give his family extra income and a chance to work at home.

Outsourcing

Taking on a craft project may require additional materials that command a specialized tool or process, such as needing handwoven fabrics for your handmade dolls. Rather than purchasing the necessary loom and related tools, you can "outsource" this work. That is, you can find another crafter who has these tools and will produce the needed components to your specifications and standards. You will save money as well as help another crafter make money at his or her craft.

If you prefer to do the work yourself, you may find a craft studio that will let you rent their equipment to produce the needed parts. There is a liability issue: Whose insurance covers you if you are injured using their equipment? Discuss this possibility with your insurance agent and make sure everyone understands the conditions.

Outsourcing specialized work is an especially profitable solution if you find yourself with a craft contract that you just can't complete on deadline. You may have the right equipment, but not enough hours in the day. You can then select a component of your work, such as making blouses for your dolls, to subcontract to another crafter. Of course, the time to select potential subcontractors is before you need them. Know who else works in your area, what they do, their skill level, and their attitude toward quality. Inspect some of their work. Then, when the big job comes in, you're ready to bid and fulfill it because you have resources.

Another resource for the outsourcer is the *Thomas Register of American Manufacturers* (Thomas Publishing), available at larger libraries. This twenty-one-volume set includes information on most manufacturers in the U.S., by category. If you decide to mass-produce some or all of your product, a manufacturer may be able to do it at a lower cost than you can do it yourself.

The Crafter's Cooperative

The idea of outsourcing specialized work leads to another opportunity you should consider: a crafter's cooperative. Crafters who don't compete with each other can reduce costs and potentially increase income by renting a large studio together and sharing some equipment and jobs. For example, a potter and a ceramicist could establish a cooperative studio and share a firing kiln, drying area and equipment, and other tools. Members of the co-op studio could go together to hire a part-time bookkeeper and even a salesperson to jointly sell their craft products.

The advantages to a crafter's cooperative are clear. The downside is the difficulty in maintaining a balanced partnership. What if the cooperating crafter gets busy and can't help you with your projects? What if you can afford to replace an important tool but the cooperating crafter cannot? Crafter's co-ops work, but they also require work.

Staying Out of Business Traps

As your craft enterprise grows, there are many business traps that you can get into. Let's look at the most common ones and how to stay out of them.

Using Credit Wisely

The biggest business trap crafters face is the credit game. For example, a new electric loom is not a necessity for making your craft. In fact, buying and using it will cost more than having fabric made. But it sure would look nice in your studio and would cost just $.92 a day! The equipment needs studio space, now at a premium. It also requires the construction of a sound-deadening room to handle the additional noise. The list goes on. What was just $.92 a day is now cutting into your profit as well as your time.

How can you escape the credit trap? By not using credit. It's difficult in this world of invoices and "put it on my account." But that's exactly what many small craft studios insist on: no credit. They say "If I can't pay cash for it, I don't need it." This may sound extreme, but many successful crafters have managed their businesses for years with this policy.

Another option is to set a more realistic credit policy: thirty days. That is, they may pick up materials from their suppliers on credit, but they pay the bill in full at the end of each month. No carry-over. No revolving credit. And they offer the same terms to their customers: payment in full within thirty days. Of course, this credit policy may limit your sales. But many crafters feel it is the only way to escape the credit trap.

Becoming Tax Savvy

Another trap all businesses face is paying excessive taxes. Once you attempt to make a profit with your craft tools and skills, the value of those tools is a legitimate expense that you can deduct from your income. Of course, some people go overboard with this and decide to deduct their living room furniture because "a customer once sat on it." Not legal! However, the shop tools you've collected over the years can be valued, then declared as a legitimate expense. As can the cost of your studio. Make sure you declare these expenses on your federal and state income taxes. I'll suggest some useful tax guides later in this chapter and tell you how to get them for free.

Purchasing Supplies

Materials used in crafts are a major component of your costs. You can reduce material costs by cooperating with other crafters to buy in quantity. This technique is especially effective for crafters who need materials offered at quantity discounts of as much as 50 percent. By learning as much as you can about other crafters in your area, their products and their material needs, you can often find someone who orders your types of materials in larger quantities and who will tack your order onto theirs. It may help them get a better price as well. Expect to pay a small fee for this service. Or, if the materials must be picked up, you can offer to pick up and deliver them in exchange for the benefits of including your materials on the order.

Know as much as you can about other crafters in your area and even your region of the country. By doing so, you may find additional opportunities for reducing material costs.

Finding Suppliers

Where can you find the right supplier? One way is by recommendations from other crafters. Another is through advertisements in crafters' magazines like *American Craft*, *The Artist's Magazine*, *Ceramics Magazine*, *Country Needlecraft*, *Decorative Artist's Workbook*, *Fiberarts*, *Lapidary Journal*, *McCall's Needlework and Crafts*, *Popular Photography*, *Woodwork*, *Workbasket* and others available at larger newsstands. For each potential supplier you want to know what supplies and materials they have available, their pricing and discounts, delivery costs and terms, return policy and minimum order requirements. You will also want to learn how knowledgeable and helpful they are. Do they understand crafts or are they just a store?

If you find two suppliers that are approximately equal sources, use them both. You then have an alternative source if prices go up. Or you may decide to give all of your business to the better supplier in exchange for an additional discount. Always have an alternate supplier.

Getting Valuable Advice for Free

As your craft business grows you will have numerous questions about keeping records, paying taxes, finding new markets, extending credit, reducing losses and locating sources for financing new equipment. Part of your tax dollars go toward funding federal and state programs that promote and help businesses.

Take advantage of these proven resources.

The Small Business Administration

Founded more than forty years ago, the U.S. Small Business Administration or SBA (1441 L Street N.W., Washington, DC 20416) has offices in one hundred cities across the U.S. and a charter to help small businesses start and grow. The SBA offers counseling and booklets on business topics, and it administers a small business loan guarantee program. To find your area's SBA office, check the white pages of metropolitan telephone books in your region under "United States Government, Small Business Administration."

The SBA offers numerous publications, services and videos for starting and managing a small business. Publications are available on products/ideas/ inventions, financial management, management and planning, marketing, crime prevention, personnel management and other topics. The booklets can be purchased for one or two dollars each at SBA offices or from SBA Publications (P.O. Box 30, Denver, CO 80201). Ask first for SBA Form 115A, *The Small Business Directory*; it lists available publications and includes an order form.

If you're already using the Internet, the Small Business Administration has a useful site for you. SBA Online can be accessed through the Internet's World Wide Web. Their location is *http://www.sbaonline.sba.gov*.

The SBA also operates the Small Business Answer Desk, a toll-free response line (800) 827-5722 that answers questions about SBA services. In addition, it sponsors the thirteen thousand Service Corps of Retired Executives (SCORE) volunteers, Active Corps of Executives (ACE) volunteers, Business Development Centers (BDCs) and Small Business Institutes (SBIs)

The Service Corps of Retired Executives (SCORE, 1441 L Street N.W., Room 100, Washington, DC 20416) is a national nonprofit association with a goal of helping small business. SCORE is sponsored by the SBA and its local office is usually in or near that of the local SBA. SCORE members (retired men and women) and ACE members (still active in their own businesses) donate their time and experience to counseling individuals regarding small business.

Business Development Centers

Business Development Centers are regional centers funded by the Small Business Administration and managed in conjunction with regional colleges. A BDC offers free and confidential counseling for small business owners and managers; new businesses; home-based businesses; and people with questions concerning retail, service, wholesale, manufacturing and farm businesses. They sponsor seminars on various business topics, assist in developing business and marketing plans, inform entrepreneurs of employer requirements, and teach cash-flow budgeting and management. BDCs also gather information sources, assist in locating business resources and make referrals.

Call your local SBA office or college campus to determine if there is a Business Development Center near you and, if so, what services they will provide as you build your craft business.

Small Business Institutes are partnerships between the SBA and nearly five hundred colleges, offering counseling services to area businesses. SBIs conduct market research, develop business and marketing plans, and help small businesses work out manufacturing problems. Contact your regional SBA office to find out if a local college has such a program. You could get free or low-cost assistance from the college's business faculty and students.

The Internal Revenue Service

The U.S. Treasury Department's Internal Revenue Service offers numerous Small Business Tax Education Program videos through their regional offices. Topics include depreciation, business use of your home, employment taxes, excise taxes, starting a business, sole proprietorships, partnerships, self-employed retirement plans, Sub-Chapter S corporations and federal tax deposits.

Here's a valuable tax tip: Depending on how much you use your business vehicle for personal use, you can either list all costs of operating the vehicle as an expense or you can deduct a standard mileage rate as an expense when you file income taxes. For more information, request *Business Use of a Car* (Publication 917) from the Internal Revenue Service. There's no charge for this publication.

What business expenses are deductible? There's a long list. The best answer is found in a free publication offered by the Internal Revenue Service, *Business Expenses* (Publication 535).

If you will have employees, you'll need to establish a payroll system. Contact the Internal Revenue Service (Washington, DC 20224) and request the *Employer's Tax Guide* (Circular E) and get a nine-digit Employer Identification Number. The IRS will then send you deposit slips (Form 8109) with your new ID number printed on them. Use these deposit slips each time you pay your payroll taxes. Payroll taxes are paid within a month of the ending of a quarter (January 31, April 30, July 31 and October 31). As your business grows, you may be required to pay payroll taxes more frequently. By then, your accountant will help you determine need and the process.

Going Online

Here's another source of free help: your computer. If you have a computer and are online with CompuServe, America Online, the Internet or another system, you can carry on long-distance conversations with other crafters. For example, CompuServe has three forums or groups for craftspeople: Handcrafts, Fibercrafts and Sewing & Quilting Forums. These groups trade information, share experiences and hold online conferences. All you need is a computer, a modem (to pass data back and forth over telephone lines), communications software (available from the online service) and a few dollars a month for online fees. If interested, talk to your friends who own computers and ask how to go online. Many colleges and computer shops also offer classes on online services.

Paying Less Taxes

Even a part-time business is required to pay income taxes on profits. Actually, you may play two roles in managing taxes. In one role, you're a debtor; in the other, an agent or tax collector. As a debtor, you're liable for various taxes and you pay them as part of your business obligations. For example, each year you owe federal income taxes which you pay out of the earnings of your business. You may also pay state income taxes on your craft profits.

As an agent, you may collect taxes and pass the funds on to a government agency. If your state requires retail sales tax on your craft products, you will collect it from your customers. Of course, if you only sell your craft on a wholesale basis, you won't have to worry about collecting and passing along sales tax. If you have employees, you deduct federal income and social security insurance (FICA) taxes, and in some states, state income taxes from the wages of your employees.

Tax Forms

If you are a proprietor, you pay your income tax as any other individual citizen: Your income, expenses and profit or loss are calculated on Schedule C, which is filed with your annual Form 1040. Partnerships and corporations use other tax forms. Self-employment tax—social security insurance for the self-employed—is reported on your Form 1040 using Schedule SE.

Individual proprietors and partners are required by law to put the federal income tax and self-employment tax liability on a pay-as-you-go basis. That is, you file a Declaration of Estimated Tax (Form 1040 ES) on or before April 15, then make payments on April 15, June 15, September 15 and January 15.

To find out more about your tax obligations, contact your regional IRS office (or call (800) 829-3676) for the following publications:

- *Tax Guide for Small Business* (Publication 334)
- *Guide to Free Tax Services* (Publication 910)
- *Your Federal Income Tax* (Publication 17)
- *Employer's Tax Guide* (Circular E)
- *Taxpayers Starting a Business* (Publication 583)
- *Self-Employment Tax* (Publication 533)
- *Retirement Plans for the Self-Employed* (Publication 560)
- *Tax Withholding and Estimated Tax* (Publication 505)
- *Business Use of Your Home* (Publication 587)

In addition, there are a number of federal forms you'll need for good record keeping and accurate taxation:

- Application for Employer Identification Number (Form SS-4) if you have employees
- *Tax Calendars* (Publication 509)
- Employer's Annual Unemployment Tax Return (Form 940)
- Employer's Quarterly Federal Tax Return (Form 941)
- Employee's Withholding Allowance Certificate (W-4) for each employee
- Employer's Wage and Tax Statement (W-2) for each employee

- Reconciliation/Transmittal of Income and Tax Statements (W-3)
- Instructions for Forms 1120 and 1120A for corporate taxes

The first publication listed is the most important—*Tax Guide for Small Business*. Request it as soon as you begin planning your business. It describes in clear language business organization, assets, profits, net income, taxes and tax forms. It also includes sample completed tax forms to follow as an example. A new edition is published each January covering the prior tax year and any important changes in the federal tax laws. Your state may have a similar publication for filing state business taxes.

Doing What You Love

Starting to sell your craft is somewhat of an experiment. It's an attempt to learn both what you want to make and what others want to buy. And, unless you have many years of experience as a crafter, you probably haven't found which type of craft you enjoy most. The message I heard from dozens of selling crafters is:

1. Find out what you love to do
2. Find someone who will pay you for doing it
3. Do it!

As you price your craft, you will also evolve as a crafter. Your product, selling strategy, personal goals and financial goals will all change. You may start out, as many crafters do, making anything people want to buy. Slowly, you'll discover what works best for you—and what doesn't. You may determine that you prefer a high-production craft, making fine jewelry or distinguished potholders. Or you may decide that you want to only produce pewter dinnerware. You search and find someone who will pay you a fair price for your skills and talents. This may take years of part-time craft to discover, during which you want to make sure your prices bring you a profit for your time. Then, possibly during a corporate downsizing, a long-term layoff or retirement, you decide it's finally time to "do it!"

Your craft has been your "escape plan" to help you through frustrating days at the job and help you afford a better life for you and your family. It offered you an outlet for your creativity. It may someday become a full-time business for you—or it may not. That's your decision. But along the way you have enjoyed what you do and helped others through your work. You have contributed to the quality of life for yourself and for others. You have been paid money for it. More important, you have been paid in personal satisfaction. And that's what being a crafter is all about.

Find a job that you really love to do and you'll never have to "work" a day in your life!

Glossary of Craft Pricing and Marketing Terms

break-even point: the point at which income equals expenses.

cash flow: the changes that increase or decrease the cash a business has.

catalog sales: selling merchandise by mail order using a catalog or related products.

commissioned crafts: crafts produced specifically for one person or company.

consignment: sales method where the dealer receives goods without purchasing them until they are sold to a customer.

craft shows: sales events designed to attract potential craft buyers to a central location.

direct sales: sales of products or services directly to the end user.

direct marketing: an attempt to sell products or services directly to the end user.

distributor: a business that purchases products for resale to retailers.

end user: the ultimate consumer or person who eventually buys a product or service.

flea market: a sales event designed to attract potential buyers of a variety of products to a central location.

indirect sales: sales of products or services to someone other than the end user.

invoice: a list of goods purchased and terms prepared by the seller for the buyer.

labor: the work required to produce a product or service.

mail-order sales: selling merchandise by mail.

manufacturer's sales representative: someone who sells products or services for the manufacturer to wholesalers or retailers on salary or commission.

marketing: the process of finding customers for your products and services.

markup: setting the retail price based on a percentage of the wholesale price.

material costs: the total cost of materials (plus shipping) required to make a product.

negotiation: the process of establishing a price that the buyer and seller agree to.

overhead costs: indirect costs of business.

packing slip: a list of goods to be shipped to a customer.

price: amount of money required to exchange a product or service.

product mix: the variety of products selected to meet the needs of a specific group of customers.

profit margin: the relationship of gross profit to net sales.

quality: the measurement against a standard.

recordkeeping: the process of tracking facts and occurrences for easy measurement and analysis.

referral sales: product sales initiated by referrals from other customers.

regional pricing: pricing based on the needs and competition within regional markets.

repeat sales: product sales earned from prior sales to customers.

retail: sales to the end user.

studio rate: the hourly rate established by a crafter to cover labor, overhead and a reasonable profit.

value: the perceived worth of all benefits of ownership.

value-added reseller: someone who adds benefits of product ownership then resells the product at a profit.

wholesale: the process of purchasing product from the manufacturer and selling it to a retailer.

YECH pricing: a pricing method that considers your costs, the economy, the competition and your need to sell (hunger).

Other terms are defined in *The Crafts Business Encyclopedia* by Michael Scott (Harvest/HBJ).

Materials Purchase Record

ITEM NUMBER	QUANTITY ORDERED	QUANTITY SHIPPED	BACK ORDERED	DESCRIPTION	DATE SHIPPED	DATE REC.	SUPPLIER

Notes:

Master copy for Material Purchase Record.

Materials Use Record

Date	
Page	of

Type of Material:

Location :

Size	Cost	How Used	Amt. Used	Value
			TOTAL	

Notes:

Master copy for Materials Use Record.

Craft Time Sheet

PERIOD END	DATE	PERSONNEL #		NAME		DIV

FOR INTERNAL USE ONLY

Description of Work	TIME DISTRIBUTION FOR PERIOD																Total Hours
	1	2	3	4	5	6	7	8	9	10	11	12	13	14	15		
	16	17	18	19	20	21	22	23	24	25	26	27	28	29	30	31	
Excused From Office																	
Holiday																	
Personal Illness - Approved																	
Overtime																	

Total Hours

List of Expenses and Dollar Value (attach receipts)

Description	$	Description	$
		Total Expenses	

Overtime Approved	Time Report

Record

Master copy for Craft Time Sheet.

Overhead Expenses

Expense	Rent & Utilities	Equipment & Tools	Supplies	Other Expenses

Master copy for Overhead Expenses form.

Inventory Record

Date	Page	of

Department :

Location:

Item#	Quantity	Description	Price	Total
			TOTAL	

Priced By:

Called By:

Checked By:

Entered By:

Master copy for Inventory Record.

Features and Benefits Worksheet

FEATURE What does it have?	BENEFIT Why is it important?

Master copy for Features and Benefits Worksheet.

Show Travel Expense Report

SHOW/LOCATION:

DATE:

To:

| DATE | TRAVELED | | MI/KM | TRANS-PORT. | HOTEL | MEALS | | | PHONE | PARKING | BOOTH EXPENSES | DAILY TOTAL |
	FROM	TO				BKFST.	LUNCH	DINNER				
TOTALS												

* EXPLANATION

Bus. MI/KM

_____ @ _____ = _____

TOTAL EXPENSE

Less Advance

Balance

☐ Claimed ☐ Refunded

CREDIT CARD BILLS

ELAPSED BUSINESS MILES/KILOMETERS

Previous Total:

Current Week:

Total to Date:

Signature of Claimant:

Approved by:

Date:

Master copy for Show Travel Expense Report.

Credit Application

BUSINESS INFORMATION	DESCRIPTION OF BUSINESS

BUSINESS INFORMATION

NAME OF BUSINESS

LEGAL (IF DIFFERENT)

ADDRESS

CITY

STATE | ZIP | PHONE

DESCRIPTION OF BUSINESS

NO. OF EMPLOYEES | CREDIT REQUESTED | TYPE OF BUSINESS

IN BUSINESS SINCE

BUSINESS STRUCTURE

☐ CORPORATION   ☐ PARTNERSHIP   ☐ PROPRIETORSHIP

☐ DIVISION/SUBSIDIARY

PARENT COMPANY _____

IN BUSINESS FOR

COMPANY PRINCIPALS RESPONSIBLE FOR BUSINESS TRANSACTIONS

NAME | TITLE | ADDRESS | PHONE

NAME | TITLE | ADDRESS | PHONE

NAME | TITLE | ADDRESS | PHONE

BANK REFERENCES

NAME OF BANK | NAME TO CONTACT

BRANCH | ADDRESS

CHECKING ACCOUNT NO. | TELEPHONE NUMBER

TRADE REFERENCES

FIRM NAME	CONTACT NAME	TELEPHONE NUMBER	ACCOUNT OPEN SINCE

CONFIRMATION OF INFORMATION ACCURACY AND RELEASE OF AUTHORITY TO VERIFY

I hereby certify that the information in this credit application is correct. The information included in this credit application is to be used to determine the amount and conditions of credit to be extended. I understand that the other sources of credit considered necessary in making the determination may also be used. Further, I hereby authorize the bank and trade references listed in this credit application to release the information necessary to assist in establishing a line of credit.

SIGNATURE | TITLE | DATE

POLICY STATEMENT: INITIAL ORDER FROM NEW ACCOUNTS WILL NOT BE PROCESSED
UNLESS ACCOMPANIED BY THE ABOVE REQUESTED INFORMATION.
TERMS: NET 30 DAYS FROM DATE OF INVOICE UNLESS OTHERWISE STATED.

Master copy for Credit Application.

Price List

Date:

No.	Code	Description	Unit Cost

Master copy for Price List.

Invoice

| Invoice: | | P.O. #: | | Date: | | Sales Rep: | |

| Sold to: | Ship to: |
| | |

Qty.	Description	Price	Total

	Subtotal	
	Sales Tax	
	Total	

Master copy for Invoice.

Packing Slip

Invoice:	P.O. #:	Date:	Sales Rep:

Sold to:

Ship to:

Qty.	Description	Price	Total

Subtotal	
Sales Tax	
Total	

Master copy for Packing Slip.

Shipping Labels

From:	From:
SHIP TO:	**SHIP TO:**

From:	From:
SHIP TO:	**SHIP TO:**

From:	From:
SHIP TO:	**SHIP TO:**

Master copy for Shipping Labels.

Phone Message

Date:	
Time:	

For: _____

From: _____

Company: _____

Number: _____

Telephoned	☐	Will Call Back	☐
Please Call	☐	Returned Call	☐

Message: _____

_____

_____

_____

_____

_____

_____

Taken By : _____

Master copy for Phone Message.

Craft Sales Record

Date	Source: Show, Phone, Contact	Craft Product(s)	Customer Information	Amount of Sale

Master copy for Craft Sales Record.

Cash Receipts

PERIOD ENDING:

Date	Check Number	Account Number	Amount	Name

Master copy for Cash Receipts form.

Cash Disbursements

PERIOD ENDING:

Date	Check Number	Account Number	Amount	Name

Master copy for Cash Disbursements form.

Master copy for Things to Do form.

Monthly Planner

PRIORITIES	Monday	Tuesday	Wednesday	Thursday	Friday	Saturday	Sunday
Week 1							
Week 2							
Week 3							
Week 4							
Week 5							

Master copy for Monthly Planner.

Cash Flow Forecast

DATE:	FOR TIME PERIOD:	APPROVED BY:
		PREPARED BY:

FOR INTERNAL USE ONLY	Date:		Date:		Date:	
	ESTIMATE	ACTUAL	ESTIMATE	ACTUAL	ESTIMATE	ACTUAL
Opening Balance						
Collections From Trade						
Misc. Cash Receipts						
TOTAL CASH AVAILABLE						

DISBURSEMENTS

Payroll						
Trade Payables						
Other						
Capital Expenses						
Income Tax						
Bank Loan Payment						

TOTAL DISBURSEMENTS						
Ending Balance						
Less Minimum Balance						
CASH AVAILABLE						

Master copy for Cash Flow Forecast.

INDEX

More Great Books for Crafters!

Crafts Marketplace: Where and How to Sell Your Crafts—Make a profit with your fine products! You'll discover more than 560 shows, craft malls, cooperatives and other places to market your work. Then, you'll be guided through every step of successfully selling your wares—from start-up through sales! #70335/$18.99/336 pages/paperback

Selling Your Dolls and Teddy Bears: A Complete Guide—Earn as you learn the business, public relations and legal aspects of doll and teddy bear sales. Some of the most successful artists in the business share the nitty-gritty details of pricing, photographing, tax planning, customer relations and more! #70352/$18.99/160 pages/31 b&w illus./paperback

The Doll Sourcebook—Bring your dolls and supplies as close as the telephone with this unique sourcebook of retailers, artists, restorers, appraisers and more! Each listing contains extensive information—from addresses and phone numbers to business hours and product lines. #70325/$22.99/352 pages/176 b&w illus./paperback

Painting Houses, Cottages and Towns on Rocks—Turn ordinary rocks into charming cottages, country churches and Victorian mansions! Accomplished artist Lin Wellford shares 11 fun, inexpensive, step-by-step projects that are sure to please. #30823/$21.99/128 pages/398 color illus./paperback

Making Greeting Cards With Rubber Stamps—Discover hundreds of quick, creative, stamp-happy ways to make extra-special cards—no experience, fancy equipment or expensive materials required! You'll find 30 easy-to-follow projects for holidays, birthdays, thank you's and more! #30821/$21.99/128 pages/231 color illus./paperback

How to Make Clay Characters—Bring cheery clay characters to life! The creator of collectible clay "Pippsywoggins" figures shares her fun and easy techniques for making adorable little figures—no sculpting experience required! #30881/$22.99/128 pages/579 color illus./paperback

The Art of Jewelry Design—Discover a colorful showcase of the world's best contemporary jewelers. This beautiful volume illustrates the skilled creative work of 21 production jewelers, featuring a wide variety of styles, materials and techniques. #30826/$29.99/144 pages/300 color illus./available 2/97

The "Make It With Paper" Series—Discover loads of bright ideas and easy-to-do projects for making colorful paper creations. Includes paper to cut and fold, templates and step-by-step instructions for designing your own creations. Plus, each paperback book has over 200 color illustrations to lead you along the way.
Paper Boxes—#30935/$19.99/114 pgs
Paper Pop-Ups—#30936/$19.99/96 pgs

Making Books by Hand—Discover 12 beautiful projects for making handmade albums, scrapbooks, journals and more. Only everyday items like cardboard, wrapping paper and ribbon are needed to make these exquisite books for family and friends. #30942/$24.99/108 pages/250 color illus.

Make Jewelry Series—With basic materials and a little creativity you can make great-looking jewelry! Each 96-page paperback book contains 15 imaginative projects using materials from clay to fabric to paper—and over 200 color illustrations to make jewelry creation a snap!
Make Bracelets—#30939/$15.99
Make Earrings—#30940/$15.99
Make Necklaces—#30941/$15.99

Handmade Jewelry: Simple Steps to Creating Wearable Art—Create unique and wearable pieces of art—and have fun doing it! 42 step-by-step jewelry-making projects are at your fingertips—from necklaces and earrings, to pins and barrettes. Plus, no experience, no fancy equipment and no expensive materials are required! #30820/$21.99/128 pages/126 color, 30 b&w illus./paperback

The Teddy Bear Sourcebook: For Collectors and Artists—Discover the most complete treasury of bear information stuffed between covers. You'll turn here whenever you need to find sellers of bear making supplies, major manufacturers of teddy bears, teddy bear shows, auctions and contests, museums that house teddy bear collections and much more. #70294/$18.99/356 pages/202 illus./paperback

How to Start Making Money with Your Crafts—Launch a rewarding crafts business with this guide that starts with the basics—from creating marketable products to setting the right prices—and explores all the exciting possibilities. End-of-chapter quizzes, worksheets, ideas and lessons learned by successful crafters are included to increase your learning curve. #70302/$18.99/176 pages/35 b&w illus./paperback

The Art of Painting Animals on Rocks—Discover how a dash of paint can turn humble stones into charming "pet rocks." This hands-on easy-to-follow book offers a menagerie of fun—and potentially profitable—stone animal projects. Eleven examples, complete with materials lists, photos of the finished piece and patterns will help you create a forest of fawns, rabbits, foxes and other adorable critters. #30606/$21.99/144 pages/250 color illus./paperback

Stencil Source Book 2—Add color and excitement to fabrics, furniture, walls and more with over 200 original motifs that can be used again and again! Idea-packed chapters will help you create dramatic color schemes and themes to enhance your home in hundreds of ways. #30730/$22.99/144 pages/300 illus.

The Complete Flower Arranging Book—An attractive, up-to-date guide to creating more than 100 beautiful arrangements with fresh and dried flowers, illustrated with step-by-step demonstrations. #30405/$24.95/192 pages/300+ color illus.

Decorative Boxes To Create, Give and Keep—Craft beautiful boxes using techniques including embroidery, stenciling, lacquering, gilding, shellwork, decoupage and many others. Step-by-step instructions and photographs detail every project. #30638/$15.95/128 pages/color throughout/paperback

Elegant Ribboncraft—Over 40 ideas for exquisite ribbon-craft—hand-tied bows, floral garlands, ribbon embroidery and more. Various techniques are employed—including folding, pleating, plaiting, weaving, embroidery, patchwork, quilting, applique and decoupage. All projects are complete with step-by-step instructions and photographs. #30697/$16.99/128 pages/130+ color illus./paperback

Nature Craft—Dozens of step-by-step nature craft projects to create, including dried flower garlands, baskets, corn dollies, potpourri and more. Bring the outdoors inside with these wonderful projects crafted with readily available natural materials. #30531/$16.99/144 pages/200 color illus./paperback

Paper Craft—Dozens of step-by-step paper craft projects to make, including greeting cards, boxes and desk sets, jewelry and pleated paper blinds. If you have ever worked with or wanted to work with paper you'll enjoy these attractive, fun-to-make projects. #30530/$16.95/144pages/200 color illus./paperback

The Complete Book of Silk Painting—Create fabulous fabric art—everything from clothing to pillows to wall hangings. You'll learn every aspect of silk painting in this step-by-step guide, including setting up a workspace, necessary materials and fabrics and specific silk painting techniques. #30362/$26.99/128 pages/color throughout